Creating Engagement between Schools and their Communities

Creating Engagement between Schools and their Communities

Lessons from Educational Leaders

Edited by Ted Purinton
and Carlos Azcoitia

LEXINGTON BOOKS
Lanham • Boulder • New York • London

Published by Lexington Books
An imprint of The Rowman & Littlefield Publishing Group, Inc.
4501 Forbes Boulevard, Suite 200, Lanham, Maryland 20706
www.rowman.com

Unit A, Whitacre Mews, 26-34 Stannary Street, London SE11 4AB

British Library Cataloguing in Publication Information Available

Library of Congress Cataloging-in-Publication Data

Names: Purinton, Ted, editor.
Title: Creating engagement between schools and their communities : lessons from educational lead-
    ers / edited by Ted Purinton and Carlos Azcoitia.
Description: Lanham : Lexington Books, [2016] | Includes bibliographical references and index.
Identifiers: LCCN 2016038713 (print) | LCCN 2016042644 (ebook)
ISBN 978-1-4985-2174-1 (cloth : alk. paper)
ISBN 978-1-4985-2175-8 (electronic)
Subjects: LCSH: Community schools. | Community and school. | Educational leadership.
Classification: LCC LB2820 .C74 2016 (print) | LCC LB2820 (ebook) | DDC 371.03--dc23 LC
    record available at https://lccn.loc.gov/2016038713.

∞™ The paper used in this publication meets the minimum requirements of American National Standard for Information Sciences Permanence of Paper for Printed Library Materials, ANSI/NISO Z39.48-1992.

Printed in the United States of America

Contents

Chapter One

What Is a Community-Focused Leader?

Ted Purinton and Carlos Azcoitia

It is now nearly unquestioned that a school leader's role is to improve classroom learning. But has something been lost as we have encouraged leaders to spend more time in classrooms? Is it possible that our increasingly narrowed educational focus on tested subjects has contributed to a far too bureaucratic and impersonal approach to educational reform? Through their very own stories, this book proposes that school leaders recontextualize their efforts within the communities from which their students reside and to reimagine, with a twenty-first-century spin, the early neighborhood-based school models that were heavily dependent upon community input and involvement, and deeply representative of local community values and customs. With such leadership, schools can once again be relevant to students and to their families and communities

Significant research demonstrates that in our drive toward higher academic achievement, we have increasingly alienated students and their families, ignored the background knowledge that students actually do have, and suppressed creativity and entrepreneurial instinct; meanwhile, we continue to watch students drop out, not attend postsecondary education, and learn that educational systems are not relevant to their lives. Perhaps centralization of curriculum (e.g., nationalized systems, Common Core, etc.) has exacerbated this, but we believe this is *not* the most fundamental cause. We assert that what matters most is how the educators within schools have actually responded: Do they pretend race and class do not matter? Do they assume that families are either engaged or not, and there is very little to do but to complain about uninvolvement? Do they act as if formal education should counteract some of the perceived negative values in certain communities? Do they, in sum, ignore the values inherent in their students' communities? What we desire is an educational leadership model that does not blame low achievement on the curricular systems, national reform mechanisms, or any-thing else that is outside the school community. As we have seen in the test score push, leaders do in fact make a huge difference. We wish, however, for leaders to make a huge difference in a more holistic sense—and ultimately to help transform their entire communities, not just their schools. We wish to see leaders who capitalize on the push for achievement with a tailored adap-tation that meets the most specific needs within the school community.

Indeed, for many decades, educational reformers have seen proposals to reconnect local communities with schools. From Dewey's beliefs about the role of schools in societies and the Freirian approaches that engage learners in political systems, to the "full-service" school models that bring clinics and social services into school buildings, there are already many examples of this sort of work out there. What is different? In our estimation, the only differ-ence is that educators are ever more divided in their time and their priorities. They must, and justifiably so, encourage increased student achievement. They are divided between the challenges of some students and ensuring equal access to high-quality education for all students in a school. The authors of this book demonstrate how schools can accomplish both goals, student achievement and community/family connections, in a way that is comple-mentary to both. And most importantly, the authors do so by showing how they, as educational leaders, were fundamentally instrumental in the process.

Traditionally, principals are considered to be mid-level managers, enact-ing within their schools what board members and political leaders demand. The school leader of the future must instead deliberately and proactively re-connect schools to their communities, creating schools that are hubs for their communities. Indeed, school leaders must still encourage achievement. Yet, the bold leader is skeptical of reform methods that assume that race, econom-ic class, family background, and so forth do not matter. The bold leader instead works closely with the community to ensure a powerful connection between all aspects of the school and the community. In sum, the bold leader brings knowledge and experience from the community into the school so that all educators involved are keenly aware of and strategically engaged in the local values, customs, challenges, cultures, and realities of school commu-nities. And the bold leader brings the school to the community in order to turn families and institutions into engaged and holistic supporters of the school mission. The point is simple: the bold leader enacts equity within communities by ensuring that the school and the community are on the same page.

The authors of this book do not engage in the tired debates about charter schools, neighborhood/district schools, magnet schools, private schools, vouchers, and so forth. Instead, the authors offer suggestions that are plau-sible for any type of school—charter or neighborhood, wealthy or poor, suburban or urban, North American or Asian. Rather than prescribing a type of "community" school, the authors offer lessons on how they achieved varied goals related to the communities in which their schools reside.

We are often told that the only way to fix a school is to shut it down and start from scratch. At the same time, school leaders are constantly expected to be tough and relentless promoters of test score improvement. But when we instead look at leaders who have stayed committed to their neighborhoods, leaders who have seen the moral imperative to provide equal opportunity to all students, we see a completely different picture of instructional leadership. This book shares those lessons, particularly from community-based schools in urban, impoverished, or immigrant communities—communities that often are disconnected from the political and economic centers of the country.

DEFINING A COMMUNITY SCHOOL

Community schools develop a culture of collaboration, manifested through particular ways of thinking and acting. Their purpose is equally to educate students and to strengthen families. They transcend cultural boundaries and build bridges by developing appropriate partnerships. They make school progress accountable to families and communities. They develop internal accountability systems with all stakeholders shifting away from political and external accountabilities. They do not follow a centralized approach where operational aspects are monitored from the outside. Rather, they value a cohesive approach by bringing people together including dissenting energy and marginalized individuals. In short, community schools push boundaries to create authenticity in partnerships and to focus on equitable schools and empowered communities.

The concept of the community school is not new. Many schools across the world have sought to increase local participation within school operations and to extend the facilities and resources of the school to community members. Perhaps with the increasing rigidity with which schools are now assessed, the concept of community schools has become more intriguing. After all, education is inherently intimate, and centralization naturally attempts to remove various layers of intimacy. Even with test-based accountability, educators have recognized the necessity of addressing social and health concerns of students and their families, in part as a way of increasing the chances that their students will attain higher academic achievement.

The community school model is not a standardized, one-size-fits-all approach to school development. There is no blueprint, no formula, no magic bullet. A community school is an idea, an aspiration, a philosophy. The more time we spend in community schools, the more we realize that the school itself is not the unit of analysis. It is the people who work in and around the school, the educators, the students, their families, the local business owners, the local religious leaders, the physicians and nurses, the concerned residents and employers—and in large part, the school leaders.

Leaders who approach the school as a hub and a central facet of the community will not need to necessarily designate their school as a "community school," though such a designation is often important to distinguish the school's philosophy. Regardless of the designation, leaders of any school can become leaders of communities by reimagining the boundaries of their work. Some leaders lament the world around their schools; they see the walls of their schools as their boundary. Other leaders engage the world beyond their walls, and as the chapters in this book will show, doing so has incredible benefits.

SITUATING COMMUNITY LEADERSHIP

We contend that community-focused school leaders approach their work with a variety of characteristics: affirmation, contribution, power, purpose, and challenge.

Affirmation

Quality community-centered schools provide a strong sense of affirmation for all members of the school community. In such communities, the school signals that individuals and groups are accepted as they are with the richness of their lives' experiences. This is in contrast to the traditional academic approach, signifying instead a sense of superiority to the community. An affirming school is a place where people care, listen, and ask questions. Most importantly, such a school does not just value the interests and perspectives of the community; it follows up with action. A leader models this by genuinely listening, by actively pursuing ideas from the community, by expressing openness to new ideas. Staff in schools may struggle to get to a point where they can affirm the experiences, lives, and values of their students and the communities in which their schools reside. Yet a community-focused school leader still should pursue such a goal. Over time, the attitude rubs off on a school's staff.

Contribution

Community schools can make a difference where valuable perspectives enrich collective endeavors for everyone's benefit. They develop a sense of connection with mutual work at the core in order to meet community goals. Human well-being becomes the norm. A community-focused school leader puts this into motion by establishing and implementing tangible programs or activities that contribute to the local community. It is not enough to talk about how a school contributes in the long-term educational sense. Indeed, we associate schools with learning, and learning takes time. A leader can demonstrate how the school contributes to all aspects of students, as well as their families and communities, by implementing specific programs and activities that are seen to directly contribute to the well-being of people.

Power

Community schools provide power with a strong sense of relevancy to daily lives and experiences. Issues are debated and choices are given so that members determine their usefulness. Community schools can guide people in a search for quality and how it can be created with the right support. How does a leader demonstrate this? Simply by giving voice to the underserved. The ballot box is a very ambiguous symbol of power; some members of the community have no access to it, while others never see results from their democratic participation. In a community institution, such as a community-focused school, however, power can be seen immediately when leaders take seriously the ideas of those who are marginalized in the community.

Purpose

Community schools clarify issues so that members understand them and see their significance. Such schools meld the cultural values of all members, create safe places for interactions, and produce results that can be witnessed across institutions, neighborhoods, and families. A community school emphasizes the continuous development of cultural proficiency to all members of the school community, not just the school staff. A leader, in particular, of a community-focused school becomes a spokesperson for reconciliation, peace, forgiveness, understanding, compassion, and love. In some sense, a community-focused leader is an activist against racism, sexism, classism, bigotry, and exploitation. Such a leader intentionally draws people together toward a common goal.

Challenge

Community schools can prepare all members to meet challenges by emphasizing internal processes of accountability—individually and collectively. They lift members to a sense of accomplishment that many people perceive as not attainable. Community schools reward self-disciplined behavior and hard work. They can bring a sense of rigor and intensity where talents and abilities are stretched (for instance, a goal of a 100 percent graduation and post-secondary enrollment). A leader does this specifically by recognizing hard work and highlighting the accomplishments of community members.

What we will see throughout this book is that community schools have become a very successful model of school organization, not necessarily because of the their label or their philosophy, but rather because of the specific actions of key people in the schools. When school leaders work toward the full inclusion of a community, and the explicit outreach of the school, they build the necessary bridges of genuine and lasting educational reform. The purpose of this book is to illustrate how community-focused leaders, most of them in schools that are labeled as community schools, do their work differently.

OVERVIEW OF THE BOOK

As you read through the chapters of this book, we challenge you to consider the ways in which schools can be transformed, through school leadership, into community hubs; and in turn, how students and their families can be affirmed and engaged. As a preview of the book, in chapter 2, the editors introduce readers to John Spry Community School in Chicago and show how, under the leadership of one of the coeditors, Dr. Carlos Azcoitia, the school became known for its academic identity. In chapter 3, Martin Blank explains how a school and its leaders provide boundary-crossing opportunities for a school to penetrate a community. In chapter 4, Chris Brown illustrates the value of school partnerships with community institutions. In chapter 5, Cincinnati Superintendent Mary Ronan looks at the entire school district and explains the impact of community school leadership at the city level. Chapter 6 is a call by Doris Terry Williams to use the community school model in the renewal of rural schools. In chapter 7, Judith Dymond presents a unique model of school-community collaboration in the pursuit of better STEM education. In chapter 8, Karen Carlson writes about the preparation of school leaders for better community-focused leadership. In chapter 9, Adeline Ray, Daniel Diehl, and Neil Naftzger describe approaches to evaluating community school leadership. As a concluding chapter, Francisco Borras, who became the second principal of the John Spry Community School, writes about succession planning, a critical issue in sustained community school leadership.

Chapter Two

Building Local Academic Identity

Ted Purinton and Carlos Azcoitia

Many educators recognize that the world of academics is quite far from the realities of their communities and families. School leaders, therefore, struggle to connect that world with the people they serve—and to demonstrate the importance of an academic culture in the school environment. Often, leaders find that they must ultimately restore a community's confidence in the educational system. Based on the experience of the authors, this chapter provides guidance on how to do that. What we will find is that no program or policy, poster or yearlong campaign, can accomplish this; it must be done through people, and the foundation must be laid with trust. Schools must be made to feel safe to the community—but not just in a physical sense; in many ways, they must be safe in an emotional and a social sense. Families need to feel welcome, not just in their presence, but also—and perhaps more so—in their participation within the academic landscape of the school.

In this chapter, by sharing the story of the John Spry Community School in Chicago's southwest side, we highlight how the role of the community-focused school leader is to shape academic identity at all levels of the community—an identity that is marked by the drive to further the place of academics in families, local businesses, places of worship, and so forth. Establishing academic identity in the community changes the paradigm of school outreach within communities by ensuring that the community seeks out its own solutions and its place within the educational system as a whole.

JOHN SPRY COMMUNITY SCHOOL

Built in 1898, John Spry Community School has served children from the Little Village community of southwest Chicago for many years. Yet, many of Spry's students would graduate in the eighth grade, get a job to help support their families, and never complete high school. In 2003, the former principal of Spry, Dr. Carlos Azcoitia, approached the district CEO about adding a high school to Spry, creating a comprehensive community school from preschool through high school. Azcoitia met with community members, parents, the local school council, teachers, and students to discuss the design of a shared community building with an innovative, "no failure" high school. Today, Spry's Community Links High School has achieved a very high graduation rate and continues to lead by example with a high number of freshmen students on track to graduation. The remainder of this chapter is based on the experiences at that school, and the knowledge gained by applying other community school models to it, and adapting lessons learned from it to other schools across the United States and internationally.

WHAT IS ACADEMIC IDENTITY AND WHY DOES IT MATTER?

First-generation college students are both heavily studied and deeply admired. They overcome huge social obstacles in order to adopt an intellectual persona and still maintain family relationships; and they face immense academic challenges in maintaining grades in spite of not having a family-based understanding of the routines and pressures of higher education (Saenz, Hurtado, Barrera, Wolf & Yeung, 2007). These troubles exist all across the world: to step into higher education is often, for many first-generation college students, to cross over into an elite world that may be perceived as out of sync with the home culture.

Consider the students, for a moment, who do not work toward any form of postsecondary education. We spend a lot of our time considering the ones who do, whether they have lengthy family histories of higher education, or whether they are the first among their family members. Often we spend considerable time worrying about the ones who are first-generation students: Will they finish? How will they relate to their families when they return home? But we do not spend as much time reflecting upon the cultures that prevent students from considering postsecondary education. What is it that holds students back? The experience of first-generation college students shows us that it is not merely the accumulation of qualifications across years of schooling. Instead, within families, communities, peer groups, and cultures or subcultures, social cues dictate individual identities that promote persistence, drive, curiosity, self-control, self-worth, and resiliency—the noncognitive factors that often influence the ultimate qualifications for higher education (e.g., Was, Al-Harthy, Stack-Oden & Isaacson, 2009). What this means is that for children and youth to be oriented toward postsecondary education, there must be multiple messages within the daily experience of students that positively encourage it. Just as a tribal culture in Southeast Asia or an elite business-minded culture in a wealthy London neighborhood may transmit multiple messages to its youth about its own values, customs, and beliefs, cultures and subcultures likewise communicate values about education, schools, postsecondary opportunities, career pathways, and so forth. In turn, such messages dictate to students and their families how to approach teacher-assigned homework, for instance. Does a student work on it straight away at 3 p.m., and postpone all television and social activity until it has been completed? Or does a student not feel any pressure to think about it until the next morning, minutes before it is due? Cultures and subcultures have a lot more to do with the level of commitment to a homework assignment than individual decision-making. Sure, a student makes decisions about how to approach homework assignments, but the decision-making is rooted in a culture that assigns a value on the task. And that value is what ultimately predisposes a student toward success within school and participation in post-secondary education in the future.

Contemporary research has two angles on this issue. On the one hand, from a psychological perspective, academic identity is a feature that instills goal orientation, and therefore, theoretically, achievement (Harackiewicz, Barron & Elliot, 1998). For instance, in one study of fifth- and sixth-grade students, researchers found that the more concerned students were with task mastery (as opposed to social or teacher recognition) the better they performed on a science activity (Meece, Blumenfeld, & Hoyle, 1988). Such performance, obviously, relates to ability to get accepted in institutions of higher education, and according to admissions officers at universities, demonstrates ability to be success with college-level work. Another study shows that those who display informational identity (e.g., thoughtful about future goals) are stronger performers than those who display diffuse-avoidant identity (e.g., not concerned with future plans) in university (Berzonsky & Kuk, 2005). Psychology obviously has a lot to say about these issues.

But on the other hand, sociological research presents a slightly different view (Hanley & Noblit, 2009). The shaping of identity does not occur in a vacuum. Identity develops as individuals negotiate, for themselves, their persona within a social context—in other words, it is how individuals want to be viewed within their respective societies. It provides the motivation for some adolescents to pursue sports and rigorous coursework, for others to pursue alternative dress and introspective personas, and for others to resort to drugs. None of these choices occur in youth as isolated, individual, noninfluenced decisions; they are intentional approaches to obtain a desired level of feedback from a chosen culture or subculture.

And the same holds true with any endeavor that connects a student to her or his school—whether academically, or even just through activities, sports, or other elements. Academic identity, simply put, is the way a student chooses to relate to school and education in pursuit of some level of acceptance by a culture or subculture, whether embodied in family, peer groups, or communities. More deeply, academic identity influences the ways in which students perceive their schools and their own educational motivations; in many ways, it is the connection they feel to their education. If it is a positive academic identity, it is a dedication to persist toward high standards (Welch & Hodges, 1997).

As a marker of academic identity, we recommend viewing the postsecondary culture within schools and communities as the best proxy. A postsecondary culture is one that prioritizes successful participation and completion in some sort of educational environment after secondary school, whether it is university, community or technical college, or something else that engages people in lifelong learning, career development, and economic and political participation. Even with primary-aged students, schools demonstrate a positive postsecondary culture by building confidence and determination in them. Achievement, though it is an essential component to postsecondary participation, is a challenging marker, as one of the most important defining elements of academic identity is a student's determination to succeed, even if that success may take years to fulfill. Low achievement can be casually and dangerously seen as a proxy for a student's motivation, or for a family's support; underneath low achievement may in fact be determination and support that allow for later success. A postsecondary culture, instead, focuses on what is possible, not on correcting what happened previously. A postsecondary culture sees daily work within schools to be preparation for the next phases of formal education, at any level. And at its root is the identity a student has as a learner. The less such an identity exists, the less likely a student will want to put in the effort—and be supported by the community and family to do so—to strive toward postsecondary education.

Throughout the chapters of this book, the various authors will suggest that academic identity is most clearly seen in schools, families, and communities based on the extent to which there is a vibrant and prevalent postsecondary culture, but academic identity can be seen in other ways, as well. Recall that a positive and healthy academic identity exists if a student identifies as a learner and feels a close connection with and investment in the educational system. Table 2.1 shows three additional ways in which it can be seen, categorized between student, family, and community.

How does a leader instill academic identity? We propose that it is a leader's job to develop a community's capacity for "self-help": to actively work toward a representative and efficient sense of ownership for the community and all its elements, including schools.

Table 2.1. Academic Identity

Ways that Academic Identity Can Be Seen	Student	Family	Community
Acknowledgment of the critical role of educational institutions in personal and societal development	Respect for school procedures and policies; positive and increasing intellectual interaction with teachers; persistence in the hard work of learning and intellectual development	Productive "teamwork" dialogue with teachers; engagement with school through learning about, discussing, and possibly debating school practices and policies	Participation in school governance; engagement with educational institutions in economic and social development; promotion of the community perception of the school
Pursuit of dialogue and learning	Interest in reading; healthy social and physical practices (e.g., exercise, healthy eating, positive friendship development); increasing ability to understand others' points of view in conflict	Modeling behaviors of reading, healthy eating, and exercise; careful monitoring of potentially racist, exclusionary, or hurtful words	Policies and practices of equity and inclusion; intolerance of racism or harassment
Self-empowerment	Resourcefulness in dealing with academic and social problems; willingness to face challenges	Modeling problem-solving skills	Vibrant local governance

HOW ACADEMIC IDENTITY WAS DEVELOPED AT SPRY

Schools cannot escape interdependence with outside factors that influence whether students learn. They must seize opportunities to connect students and families to resources and support, rather than lament the prevalence of outside negative influences. Spry developed a variety of approaches to seize those opportunities. We describe just a few of those approaches here:

- *Signaling quality.* Even neighborhood students were required to submit an application for admission to the school. We interviewed families and shared through that process our expectation that they demonstrate commitment to the school and to its objectives.

- *Meaningfully extending the school day.* Rather than add more academic class time, or watching our students spend time on the streets in the afternoon, we provided opportunities for students to capitalize on their strengths and interests. Our after-school activities built on their social and recreational interests and accommodated various learning needs and styles. This gave us an opportunity to interact with our students in a casual, and in some regard, playful manner.
- *Expanding access to learning.* We offered family and community courses for high school equivalency, English, and literacy; and often we even customized courses that reflected particular neighborhood needs. These courses were expensive for us to run, as they were not reflected in our regular budget, but the cost was negligible in comparison to the gain it provided for the interaction we had with the community.
- *Partnering with the right agencies.* A partnership with a health agency allowed Spry to offer health fairs, conferences, and services to families. This collaboration culminated with the opening of a school-based clinic.
- *Sitting down for coffee.* We instituted home gatherings for parents that emphasized financial education, neighborhood improvement, immigration rights, and community safety. This allowed us to see the community as it was, and it allowed the community to see us as advocates, not bureaucratic authorities.
- *Sleeping in.* Because teenagers respond better when they begin their classes later in the day, we instituted a flexible high school schedule. This permitted a wide range of opportunities for students before school, if they wished to show up earlier.
- *Finishing early.* In traditional high schools, if students are caught in a syndrome of failure, summer school is often used to make up failed classes. Our model, instead, allowed students to attend school year-round and complete college entrance requirements in three years. Students and families make a commitment to complete high school and enroll in a post-secondary school; starting their first year of high school, students visit colleges and universities. During their third year, they all participate in dual-enrollment programs for college and high school credit. This intensive approach never gave our students the chance to fall behind: they were so busy keeping up that they barely noticed high school finished so fast.

Though this list could continue for pages, it provides a glimpse at how we saw ourselves in relationship with our community. What we wanted to do, ultimately, is give families and our students tools by which to help themselves: we called it "building capacity for self-help."

BUILDING CAPACITY FOR SELF-HELP

In the well-known words of Confucius, "Give a man a fish and he will eat for a day. Teach a man to fish and he will eat for a lifetime." This is our view of educational reform. A focus on improving a student's test scores will result in improved test scores. Yet a broader focus on changing the way families and communities approach formal education, and how schools approach families and communities to recruit them in the effort toward broader educational gains, will have a very different approach. We call this *self-help*, and as leaders, a central goal should be to develop that capacity within all school stakeholders. The purpose is to ensure that all stakeholders are holding up their end of the responsibility in the educational mission. No teacher or principal can accomplish lasting learning gains when students and their families are not convinced that hard academic work is essential; and so instead of complaining about the challenge, when leaders build the capacity for self-help, they are re-creating the environments within the community necessary to support lasting learning gains. The community is best served when capacities are developed so that people can help themselves.

At the heart of self-help is ownership of the educational mission. All community institutions can be included—local businesses, places of worship, community organizations, city government, families, and social services. The purpose of building such capacity within all of these institutions is to ensure that the community supports academic identity within students by connecting for the whole community the role that knowledge, skill, disposition, creativity, entrepreneurship, and citizenship play in success and enjoyment in all other aspects of a community.

Consider events a few years ago in the school districts of Washington, DC, and Chicago: certain schools were underenrolled and/or low performing; district officials moved to close those schools down; and parents, as well as entire communities, protested in complete shock at such decisions. In 2012 in New York City, when specific low-performing schools were slated for "turnaround" status—meaning, the principal would be replaced, teachers would likely face replacement, and a whole new staff would run the school—parents reported anger, depression, and resentment. Students were distraught as teachers they trusted were swiftly removed. New teachers took significant time to get up to speed with the local cultures.

What happened? Could this upheaval have been prevented? According to many parents and community members in those districts, the extent to which their schools were considered low performing was unknown. Indeed, it does seem fairly reasonable that principals failed to bring this reality up to parents; after all, it is hard to tell parents that their children may be going to a troubled school. The repercussions may seem more personal when sharing the news with parents than with dealing with the bureaucratic pressures of a school district central office or a state department of education. But it also may be plausible that *not* addressing the failing school status with parents might have prevented improvement from occurring. If families are not on board with the habits that are most closely associated with strong achievement, gains may be hampered or at best only marginally better. Many successful charter school networks use this approach with individual families. What a successful community school leader does, however, is attempt to extend the ethos of postsecondary achievement throughout all aspects of the community so that it permeates nearly every place of interaction with families and students. The leader promotes the engagement of students by engaging the entire community; the entire community can be leveraged to support students as effective learners. The most important habits associated with strong achievement do not develop in the vacuum of a school; they are supported entirely through every form of influence in a student's life.

Leadership research and theory bears this out. Whether for good or bad, school leaders (and leaders of most types of organizations, for that matter) act as intermediary players—between the organizations and the people those organizations serve (Weick, 1976). They "translate" the wishes, concerns, and realities of their organizations (in this case, teachers and school staff members) to the people that schools serve (students, parents, board members, communities, politicians); and at the same time, they "translate" the wishes, concerns, and realities of the people that schools serve to the teachers and staff members within the schools. In some cases, principals can behave (either intentionally or unintentionally) as bottlenecks, holding back information from either side; and in other cases, they behave as spokespeople for the other side.

In building a school community marked by self-help, the principal, though still a major intermediary player, becomes less of one. Open communication between parents, board members, politicians, community leaders, students, teachers, and staff becomes a hallmark of the school. People understand what it takes to improve and what is at stake; and most importantly, they are part of the solution.

The question remains, though: How does a principal make this happen? Before we discuss actual steps, we want to provide a framework for what a community-focused principal actually does—in other words, the goal of various steps and actions taken by a principal. In sum, we suggest that a principal creates accountability within the community, but does so in a relational way, not in the traditional bureaucratic way.

Relational accountability in community schools is fostered by creating bonds among students, families, school staff, and community members to advance the mission of the school and address the common good. Empowerment addresses the fact that many individual problems are affected by larger forces, so students must become socially responsible by participating in community organizing initiatives. Students learn to make a difference and develop leadership skills as they participate in community projects. What can be done becomes real. The perception of the school begins to change and the educational agenda becomes stronger. All members of the school community become co-producers of a movement to make the school and the community better. They also push boundaries to address equity and excellence in order to create a socially just school community driven by strategies and action. All members transcend cultural boundaries to develop reciprocal accountability.

John Spry Community School became the catalyst for bringing together other schools, community organizations, and other public services to organize for peace. Students were members of the organizing team to conduct peace marches. High school students not only tutored primary students in the primary program but also participated in internships in neighborhood organizations and businesses. Saturday housing fairs were conducted with banks at the school so families could learn the intricacies of loan and mortgage applications for purchase and remodeling. Community gatherings were held in the school auditorium to address quality-of-life issues such as delays in street repaving and repairs. Students, parents and community members compiled data to address the need for a public library in the community based on the number of elementary and high school students in the area. A new library was built after testimonies were provided to the commissioners. A public garden is envisioned for students and families and strategy sessions were conducted at the school. A scholarship fund was established to help families with tuition costs for postsecondary education as well as assistance for undocumented students.

In sum developing the capacity for self-help with results became a priority for the community.

ENACTING RELATIONAL ACCOUNTABILITY

In a review of research on education-related community organizing, M. Elena Lopez (2003) lays out four key goals that community organizers can work toward as they seek to empower families and communities to pursue academic excellence within local schools:

- Focus on parental concerns
- Develop parental leadership
- Build social capital
- Mobilize collective power (in other words, help parents focus on how they can participate in public accountability)

These four goals show us that empowerment is a collective responsibility: it does not happen by just convincing people that they can step up and lead. In many ways, being empowered is recognizing that we choose our own attitudes to improve circumstances instead of lamenting the influence of outside factors that impede progress. But to move a community toward empowerment, we need to recognize why empowerment has not occurred in many of our communities: Frequently, our systems have alienated citizens and participants for political, racial, economic, bureaucratic, religious, and social reasons. People have been disempowered because they do not recognize how being empowered will make any difference—in other words, empowerment often comes across as mere rhetoric. And as we discussed in regard to academic identity, alienation from a system may very well indeed shape personas and identities that are contrary to school: if a family is alienated from academic culture, why would that family feel the desire to continue pursuing it? That family will instead pursue other goals that are more attainable. Thus, principals have two interrelated tasks:

1. School leaders must restore the relationship between families and communities with educational institutions that for so long have been viewed as oppressive, irrelevant, or impersonal.
2. School leaders must build a sense of confidence in people and demonstrate that they have a key role in the life of the school.

We do these things by enacting relational accountability. Bureaucratic accountability mechanisms, which run most of our educational system, seek to depersonalize responsibility and feedback. Despite bureaucracy's negative connotation, this has not always been a bad thing. Bureaucracy, in its most fundamental sense, has sought to provide greater structure and stability to public services—reducing, in effect, the negative impact of nepotism, favoritism, favors, and so forth (Wilson, 1991). With a depersonalized system, one school in a district should theoretically know how it will be measured relative to another one.

Yet clearly this has had a detrimental effect in so many other ways. Bureaucratic school systems have overemphasized numbers, criteria, credentials, policies, and regulations. Though this has reduced corruption and increased accountability meant to provide transparency in providing equitable access, it has not had a major impact on increasing educational professionalism, which relies on individual educator judgment; it has reduced achievement problems to a mere blanket explanation of "failure." And it does not promote the sort of individual level of responsibility that is so critical at all levels in any educational system (Purinton, 2011).

By instead promoting relational accountability, a school leader seeks to connect people in a way that allows individual strengths to flourish. If building an academic identity within a student body (and by extension, within the entire community) is an essential step, as we have just described, it is incumbent upon the educational professionals within the school to understand how that can be accomplished. Assuredly, it cannot be done with simple solutions, such as packaged programs or isolated events; educators will have to dig deep within the community to in turn find what the community has to offer and how that can be adapted into an academic identity.

We therefore suggest three essential steps that can help in enacting relational accountability:

1. Turn on.
2. Tune in.
3. Get out.

Turn On

Schools spend considerable time trying to figure out how they can improve their internal processes; as we would and should expect, schools want to improve what society expects of them: the education of children and youth through, mainly, classroom-based learning activities. However, schools have many resources that are rarely tapped outside the schoolhouse walls. So, the first step in establishing a positive academic identity in the community, and in building a culture of self-help through relational accountability, is to identify the school's strengths and weaknesses as a community institution, not just an educational one. In other words, a school should conduct a self-assessment, answering the following essential question: *How trustworthy are we?* There is no sense in leading the community if the school cannot offer it anything. The following questions must be addressed in this self-assessment:

When we are alone, how do we talk about our families and our community? This is a critical question, one that could easily be answered dishonestly. What a school must do in answering this question is to evaluate the predominant underlying views of its families and community so that it can assess its own attitudes. The only trouble with this question is that it is quite possible that the educators in a school may rationalize their views ("We don't look down on the families in our community, but we just wish they would care more about their children by participating more.") or see the question as threatening. In such situations, it is important for the principal to bring the situation to the school's attention on a regular basis. For instance, the school can celebrate one asset of its community each month during a school year. A technique utilized in an increasing number of schools is home visits, whereby teachers visit a couple families throughout the academic year. Of course, this is seen by families as reaching out, but the greatest value may actually be in a teacher getting an up-close understanding of how their students experience life.

What skills and resources does this school have that could be used by the community? Most schools have computers, libraries, athletic facilities, and so forth. Before seeking resources to add new elements to the school (e.g., medical clinics, etc., which will be discussed in a later chapter), schools should evaluate what they already do have. One school's computer teacher, who carried no teaching load in the first two hours of each day, recognized that he could put on parent workshops for utilizing Google Docs in the computer laboratory. At another school, the basketball courts sat empty on the weekends, and so the PE teachers opened them up and found enough money to pay for a custodian to unlock and lock the courts up at the beginning and end of the weekend days. Surely teachers have skills and competencies that could be utilized outside the regular classroom; those resources should, at the very least, be identified.

What is the history of the school within the community? This question may take some time to appropriately answer, particularly if the staff is on the newer side. But it is important to understand how the school has been viewed within the community over time. Details such as labor strikes, tragedies (e.g., a student or teacher death that got a lot of local attention), popular (or unpopular) past teachers and principals (e.g., school heroes or villians), and major construction projects can provide clues to how the community views the school. This is the sort of question that cannot be answered simply with public perception surveys, for instance; the deepest historical roots are not necessarily explicit parts of the community culture forever; instead, they make up the essence of the school within the community, and for longtime residents, there need be no utterance of actual events, as they, over time, constitute the "whole" that is now understood. But of course, the educators in the school, if new, may not actually know these things. It is critical, therefore, to get that sense. The institution, simply put, outlasts the people, and therefore, it is a mistake for educators to view their role at a school as being outside the course of the institution's wider history.

What is the educational background of the community? This is a seemingly simple question that most educators already understand about their schools. Yet, there is a deeper implication in this question. Educators must understand how various cultural or minority groups have assimilated into the educational system at large.

These questions all naturally lead to possible action, but it would be a mistake to simply take action. Indeed, that is what schools often do. But perhaps some of the problem schools face in relating to their communities is that educators listen to themselves only. So, the next step is to "tune in."

Tune In

Communities contain cultures. Educators often forget that the cultures of the communities they work in may be different from their own cultures. And when cultures differ, values do, as well. How do leaders, then, get a sense of the local community cultures? Many schools have instituted home visitations as a way to better understand their communities. While this is a very good idea, it can also be quite time consuming. Often, the best way to manage this is to do it sporadically. Here, we suggest some additional steps that any school can implement:

Educational block clubs. Similar to any other sort of block party, where groups of people in a particular neighborhood join together in a living room over coffee, an educational block club is a venue for discussion about educational issues. Teachers can volunteer to participate over discussions related, in particular, to literacy, health, safety, and other pressing concerns for families. Or principals, themselves, can get involved in each club. Either way, these should be considered by educators as venues for parents or community members to freely express their views.

Family Conference Series. With the expertise of community representatives, teachers, and others, schools can put on short interactive lectures with follow-up discussions. Topics can include nutrition, family field trips, family reading, child development, social and emotional development, health, self-esteem, communication with adolescents, homework and so forth. Topics can come directly from parents. Participants who attend can receive certificates of completion. It is important to not patronize parents, so one way to manage this is to have them present when feasible. Though lectures are not necessarily "listening" activities, doing such a thing opens the door for conversation. The topics parents show interest in can be a clue to what is important.

Student & Family Interviews. At the beginning of the school year, principals and teachers people "interview" parents and students, not as a way to "test" their qualifications, but instead to learn about them. Some principals we know use the strategy of asking parents to tell them everything they want the school to know about their student.

Spending time in community. How many principals and teachers come to the neighborhoods in which they work on the weekend? For breakfast at local restaurants? Mid-morning visits to coffee shops? Attending religious services?

We could continue for many more pages with ideas, and readers surely have their own. But the point is simple: leaders can learn about their communities and families in order to *tune their messages*. Message tuning is critical in a leadership role, as described previously in this chapter, because leaders of any type of organization are inherently the key messengers between their organizations and the organization's clients/customers/participants/students. Principals translate messages from the community (as well as from school boards, school district administrative offices, parents, and so forth) to the school, and vice versa. But school leaders, and educators in general, do not always come from the communities in which they work; therefore, they have to work quite hard to truly understand the values and cultures of their school communities. The leader who can speak toward those values and within that culture will of course be heard by the community more clearly. Not only will the community see value in a better tuned message (i.e., they can respect a leader who has taken the time to care), the conversation will be more mutual. If principals talk from their experiences, and families have different ones, the underlying values of such simple issues as homework, reading habits, and postsecondary pursuits will not translate well. As one study showed, the "be true to yourself" mantra in management is actually not effective: leaders who adapt to those around them ("chameleons") tend to be more successful in their endeavors (Kilduff & Day, 1994). We cannot pretend we are people we are not, but we can learn how best to work within the communities where we work.

Get Out

Finally, once we have sought insight from our communities, and listened to it deeply—enough to change how we talk about education and our schools— we must get out there into the community and demonstrate that we know and genuinely believe our schools are not always the central focal points of our communities. For many communities, it is the places of worship that form the central backdrop to community identity; in others, cultural venues, shopping malls, or public spaces are central meeting points and community identifiers. In many modern communities, such focal point locations may not even exist, as people increasingly isolate themselves from their neighbors. Nonetheless, it is critical for school leaders—and, in fact, all educators—to get out, be seen, and integrate within the communities where they work.

Chapter Three

Boundary-Crossing Leadership for Community Schools

Martin Blank

John Gardner's (1993) call for boundary-crossing leadership has become more resonant in many different sectors in the more than twenty years since it was first written: "In a tumultuous, swiftly changing environment, in a world of multiple colliding systems, the hierarchical position of leaders within their own system is of limited value because some of the critical tacks require lateral leadership—boundary crossing leadership—involving groups over whom they have no control" (p. 98). His approach has emerged slowly in the education space, which led many schools to focus narrowly on academic achievement under the No Child Left Behind Act.

The new Elementary and Second Education Act, now labeled Every Student Succeeds Act, changes the accountability equation. States are now required to include at least one measure that goes beyond academics in their accountability frameworks. Possibilities include student engagement, educator engagement, school climate/safety, or students' opportunity to learn.

This is a welcome development for educators, advocates, community leaders, and community partners who believe that closing the opportunity gap and addressing inequities in students' lives are essential to closing the achievement gap. The realities of young people's lives bear out the need to broaden the way leaders think and act as they seek to prepare our young people to thrive in the twenty-first century.

Poor children and children of color experience higher rates of chronic absence and lower levels of third-grade reading scores (Chang & Romero, 2008). There are significant disparities in rates of suspension and expulsion for this group (Losen & Skiba, 2010), as well as correlations between academic performance and vision problems, asthma, teen pregnancy, aggression, and violence. Moreover, research shows that low-income families can afford to spend far less on offering enrichment experiences to their children (Duncan & Murnane, 2014). Beyond this we know that toxic stress and the sense of isolation that comes from growing up in racially and economically segregated neighborhoods influence student success.

All of this is true at a time when we have a student population that is more than 50 percent poor and increasingly diverse, with the percentage of English language learners continuing to grow (Southern Education Foundation, 2015). The number of languages spoken and cultures present in public schools continue to challenge a predominantly white teacher workforce.

All of these challenges walk through the schoolhouse door each day, but schools today have neither the expertise nor resources to address them. Their leaders must, as John Gardner urged, become boundary-crossing leaders— leaders who reach out and build deep, intentional, and sustained partnerships with other organizations over which they have no control. Why? To get the results our nation seeks for its young people.

There are more than 150 school districts implementing the community school strategy. They cut across the nation, from New York to Chicago; from Evansville to Lincoln to Salt Lake, and in Oakland, San Francisco, and Hayward, California. Small, medium, and large districts are in the mix. Building on the experience of the past twenty years, the potential for growth is significant, particularly with a new law that opens up additional flexibility for local school districts.

What is the vision for a community school that has such relationships? How are leaders organizing themselves to guide the development and implementation of community schools? And finally, what is the know-how that school leaders need to lead community schools, and how do we get the leaders we need? This chapter begins to answer some of these questions.

THE COMMUNITY SCHOOL: A PARTNERSHIP-DRIVEN VISION FOR OUR PUBLIC SCHOOLS

Since 1997, the Coalition for Community Schools has advocated for schools as centers of flourishing communities where everyone belongs, works together, and thrives. We define a community school as both a place and a set of partnerships between the school and other community resources. It has an integrated focus on academics, health and social services, youth and community development, and community engagement that leads to improved student learning, stronger families and healthier communities.

Community schools seek to create the conditions necessary for children and youth to learn. Consider these "conditions for learning" taken from the Coalition for Community Schools (2005):

- Early childhood development is fostered through high-quality, comprehensive programs that nurture learning and development.
- The school has a core instructional program with qualified teachers, a challenging curriculum, and high standards and expectations for students.
- Students are motivated and engaged in learning—both in school and in community settings—during and after school.
- The basic physical, mental, and emotional health needs of young people and their families are recognized and addressed.
- There is mutual respect and effective collaboration among parents, families, and school staff.
- Community engagement, together with school efforts, promotes a school climate that is safe, supportive, and respectful and connects students to a broader learning community.

From a community school perspective, fulfilling these conditions requires deep, respectful, and purposeful relationships among educators, families, and community partners. Local government, higher education institutions, United Ways, community-based organizations, and neighborhood and faith-based groups all have important contributions to make.

These partnerships ultimately help build and integrate three common elements of a community school: (1) health and social supports for students and families, often called wraparound services; (2) authentic family and community engagement; and (3) expanded learning opportunities inside and outside the school that support the core curriculum and enrich students' learning experiences. For school and community leaders, community schools are not a "silver bullet" but rather are a strategy for developing collective trust, action, and impact.

In *Our Kids*, Robert Putnam (2015) suggests that America no longer sees itself as having shared responsibility for the education of all its children. Community schools are an antidote to that attitude.

Results-focused partnerships are the foundation for community schools. Local leadership typically focuses on broad results that matter to multiple stakeholders. Here is a list of broad results that community schools seek:

- Children are ready to enter school
- Students attend school consistently
- Students are actively engaged in learning and in their community
- Families are increasingly involved in their children's education
- Students are healthy—physically, socially, and emotionally
- Students live and learn in safe, supportive, and stable environments
- Communities are desirable places to live
- Students graduate ready for college, career, and citizenship

A careful analysis of each result, and the related indicators for measuring progress, makes clear that schools need their community to move the needle on specific issues. For example, chronic absence is not just a school issue; its cause is often embedded in health and family issues. Making sure students are healthy often entails relationships with health and mental health organizations. And a focus on student engagement might involve partnerships with arts and cultural institutions, museums, or environmental and hunger groups among others.

BOUNDARY-CROSSING LEADERSHIP STRUCTURES

At the community or school district level, networks of boundary-crossing leaders such as superintendents, elected officials, United Ways, local government, higher education institutions, health systems, community-based organizations, and other community partners work together to drive the community school vision forward. In addition to communicating a shared vision, these groups are responsible for developing supportive policy, mobilizing and aligning community resources, and outlining accountability plans to build and sustain a system of community schools. Put differently, the job of a community leadership group is to create the conditions for educators and their partners to help young people thrive.

Superintendents and central office personnel often interact with leaders of other major community institutions on a formal or informal basis. For school leaders the challenge is to turn a board role or an informal relationship into a strategic partnership with organizations they do not control.

Consider United Ways, whose national goals of improving health, education, and incomes fit well with the community school strategy (United Way, 2015). The United Way of Salt Lake, for example, is a major driver of community schools in its region. A growing number of higher education institutions are engaging in university-assisted community schools which bring the assets of a university or college together to support nearby public schools.

In the local government sector, cities and counties are increasingly becoming involved with community schools. New initiatives are emerging in Newark and Philadelphia, and New York City is financing a major expansion. An exemplary county is Multnomah County, Oregon, which, in partnership with the city of Portland and six participating school districts, is now organizing 81 SUN Community Schools (School Uniting Neighborhoods).

A strong community leadership group at the district or city level ensures that community schools are aligned with the district's vision for better learning and student success. Superintendents are important participants in these groups, but they need not necessarily be in charge. By giving greater public roles to community partners, within the parameters of a shared vision, school leaders can better influence gathering community assets to support critical education outcomes. Established relationships are ideally turned into formal agreements enabling partners to hold each other accountable and help avoid miscommunication about respective roles, resource sharing, and program quality and effectiveness.

The school-site leadership team, another boundary-crossing leadership structure, is important at the school level. Schools often have community partners, but in too many cases no agreed-upon strategy or set of desired results. Partners run programs that are good for students but not intentionally linked to the core mission of the school. A strong site leadership team addresses this challenge.

Principals, teachers, and other school staff work together with parents and community partners to develop a strategy for their school through the site leadership team. They are responsible for needs assessment, planning, and implementation, as well as the alignment of educators and partners toward a common set of results and communicating with the broader school community. The team incorporates partners' assets into the school-wide plan and advocates for outstanding assets.

This team need not be a new committee. Existing school groups now focused on school decision making, student support, health, or other issues could take a broader role. What is essential is that educators, families, and community partners have a venue for thinking together about the results they want for their children and that they continuously review their efforts in order to improve quality and enhance impact.

A community resource coordinator is a key dimension of the community school strategy. Also referred to as resource coordinator, community school director, or site manager, the community resource coordinator is a new leadership role in our public schools. This individual serves as the bridge between the school and the community, facilitating the work of the site leadership team, leveraging community partners, and integrating their assets and expertise into the life of the school.

The coordinator job demands an individual whose skills cross many disciplinary boundaries—part social worker, community development and organizing specialist, educator, and planner. Hiring a coordinator from a partner organization demonstrates the school's commitment to tapping local expertise. A coordinator serving on the school leadership team ensures that community resources are fully part of the conversation and add the most value to the school.

Across the country various funding sources feed into community school coordinator costs: local school funds, federal and state grants, foundation and community partner funds. Research and experience suggest that once principals have the support a community coordinator brings to their school, they find resources in their own budget to cover the costs. Diversified funding in community schools leverages a return on district dollars invested at a ratio of at least 3:1 (Blank, 2010). Other principals have generated totals over $10 and as high as $20 (Martinez & Hayes, 2013).

Gluing together the work of the community school leadership team and the school site groups is an intermediary. This entity keeps the whole enterprise moving. It may be an organization, a school district, United Way, city, or higher education institute. It often includes a working group composed of key managers from partner agencies. The intermediary provides planning, coordination, and management support, facilitates communication among community-wide and school-site leaders, and works to measure progress. Central office school district staff often participate in these intermediary efforts since they are best able to help community partners understand how the school systems function, work through specific issues, and recommend changes in the school district that might make partnership with the community easier; these may include data sharing, security, and custodial issues. These cross-boundary leadership structures unite and mobilize community assets for the community school.

Here are some good examples of how boundary-crossing leadership results in innovative school environments.

Community Learning Centers, Cincinnati, Ohio

Recognizing the fundamental connections among student health, readiness to learn, and academic achievement, Cincinnati's Community Learning Centers (CLCs) partner with the Cincinnati Health Department through the Growing Well Health Collaborative to coordinate school-based health services. There are thirty-five CLCs with a resource coordinator in each school. Cincinnati Public Schools, the Greater Cincinnati United Way, and local foundations provide leadership for the effort with support from the Community Learning Centers Institute, local intermediary groups, and district staff. One of their CLCs, Oyler School, has received national attention for building one of the largest CLCs. It includes a school-based health center providing primary, dental, and vision care, an Early Learning Center, and a community mental health provider.

Schools Uniting Neighborhoods, Multnomah County, Oregon

Results-focused partnerships are essential to the community school strategy in Multnomah County, Oregon. The countywide Schools Uniting Neighborhoods (SUN) initiative includes eighty-five community schools across six districts, each with a lead community partner. The SUN Coordinating Council, including leadership from the county, the city of Portland, a major funding partner, and six participating districts, drives the SUN schools. SUN's intermediary, the county human services department, ensures that all partners and schools are collaborating toward results through annual plans specifying how they will work together to increase learning opportunities, implement strategies that promote better attendance, and provide health and other services to students and families. In their agreement partners must describe which strategies they will employ to boost reading, math, writing, or attendance, as well as what indicators they will use to measure progress. These plans are required by contractual agreements at multiple levels signed by the intermediary, school district, principal, and lead partner agency.

Learning Partnerships in Practice, Albuquerque, New Mexico

Albuquerque's Community Schools Partnership is a unique arrangement between the Albuquerque Public Schools, the city of Albuquerque, and Bernalillo County. This partnership invested in a director for community schools who reports to a leadership board including these partners and members of the business and nonprofit communities. There are now twenty-three community schools in Albuquerque. One special program to get parents into the school and supporting their child's learning is Homework Diners. The idea is simple: offer parents an opportunity to come into the physical school building and work with teachers and community partners on what children are learning in the classrooms, while eating a provided dinner. Parents connect with teachers in an informal way and check on their student's progress. Children see how much parents care about their learning, and parents have the supports on-site to help them help their children.

United Way of Salt Lake, Salt Lake City, Utah

The Granite School District is one of four that are part of United Way of Salt Lake's Promise Partnership Community School Initiative using community schools as the vehicle. The United Way of Salt Lake organized its community schools within specific communities, using the Promise Neighborhood Initiative as a model.

The Collective Impact approach created far-reaching, systemic change that supports and is bolstered by the work on the ground. The cradle-to-career framework also meant that United Way would refocus its efforts on developing a pipeline of services in specific communities—combining the strengths of the community school strategy with a place-based initiative. United Way employs school directors (community school coordinators) who are considered key members of the school leadership. In addition to monthly meetings with partners, the directors convene biweekly. They also have pipeline meetings to examine data on students transitioning between schools and focus on how services can follow them. This continuity is exemplified by the mobile health clinic that Utah Partners for Health brings to participating schools. The medical staff provide checkups, women's health exams, and primary health care to uninsured and underinsured families.

A Promise Partnership Regional Council guides the initiative and focuses on keeping the work aligned. It formed in 2014 and includes education, business, government, and nonprofit leaders. Collaborative Action Networks have also been formed to organize the work and bring partners together around specific goals. Convening around a desired result—such as improving third-grade reading scores or increasing the percentage of high school students who are college ready—is different than convening around a program or a funding stream and unites providers who otherwise never work together.

WHAT LEADERS FOR COMMUNITY SCHOOLS NEED TO BE ABLE TO DO

Most of the recent literature on school leadership focuses on management and technical aspects and instructional leadership. While important, that skill set may not be at the heart of school leadership requirements.

John Gardner shared a set of leadership attributes that continues to resonate. With a constituency that includes students, parents and families, civic and business leaders, teachers, paraprofessionals, community partners, faith-based and community-based groups, and volunteers, a school leader guiding a community school must think and act more like a leader in the broadest sense. Eight of those attributes reflect particular responsibilities relevant to school leaders (Gardner, 1993, chapter 5):

- *Intelligence and judgment—in action.* School leaders must not only be knowledgeable and smart, they must all be able to act in a thoughtful way.
- *Understanding of follower constituents and their needs.* School leaders must understand the various constituencies with whom they work—their teachers, paraprofessionals, family, community partners and students.
- *Working with diverse groups.* The demographic changes in the country demand school leaders who are comfortable moving in different cultures and are able to listen and understand the different perspective that people bring.
- *Knowledge of other systems and institutions.* To tap the assets and expertise of other groups, school leaders should understand their mandates and interests and how they connect with the mission of public schools.
- *Skill in dealing with people.* For school leaders this means having the social and emotional skills needed to appraise accurately the readiness or

resistance of followers to move in a given direction and to know when discussion or confusion is undermining the group's will to act.

- *Capacity to motivate.* This idea is at the heart of the popular notion of leadership, and school leaders must have the ability to move the entire school community to action and results.
- *Courage, resolution, steadiness.* School leaders need courage and the ability to risk again and again in order to help young people succeed.
- *Adaptability and flexibility.* The problems that come to the door of our public schools demand leaders who can adapt to an ever-changing environment and shift quickly from a failing tactic to another approach.
- *Physical vitality and stamina.* Oft overlooked, this quality will surely resonate with school leaders who have long days, including weekends, with challenging issues and difficult decisions that tax them physically and emotionally.

The broad attributes of leadership must of course be melded with the unique knowledge and skills needed to lead and work in a public school environment. The *2015 Professional Standards for Educational Leadership* are a valuable step forward, reflecting more specifically on characteristics of a school leader. The Standards focus on equity and cultural responsiveness, community of care and support for students, and meaningful family and community engagement.

Combining Gardner's attributes with these new standards offers real promise for developing the kinds of boundary-crossing leaders we need for community schools. But for community schools to work, leadership development must not only focus on principals, but on teachers, community school coordinators, professionals in related fields, and parent leaders too.

Teachers generally say they learned a little about working with families and next to nothing about the community during their training. Given the research on the importance of family engagement in the education of children (e.g., Henderson & Mapp, 2002) and the *Dual Capacity Building Framework for Family School Partnerships* issued by the Department of Education (Mapp & Kuttner, 2013), this is indeed short-sighted. The new Every Student Succeeds Act includes an emphasis in this area for teachers as well as principals and must be mined.

We also need institutions of higher education to initiate programs training community school coordinators. Such a curriculum would integrate knowledge from education, social work, and community organizing, youth development, and strategic planning and management. This level of professional preparation is essential to grow the thousands of necessary community school coordinators. Right now local initiatives are preparing their own staff through in-service training or through relationships with technical assistance groups such as the National Center for Community Schools. This is required but not sufficient. We need far more interdisciplinary programs to prepare people to bridge schools and communities. The University of Chicago School of Social Services Administration Leadership in Community Schools Program has been a leader in this regard.

Interdisciplinary preparation for individuals entering specific professional occupations is needed as well. Future professionals in the fields of health, counseling, social work, criminal justice, and education now rarely have shared experiences during their professional preparation. Yet they will often interact on the job, and particularly in community schools. Joint classes and experiences that help people develop a shared language and understanding of the culture of different systems, and what good interdisciplinary practice looks like in a real school setting, would set the stage for more and better collaboration to support students.

Everyone can be a leader in a community school, and this proposition must include parents and families. Their voices are vital in community schools if family and community engagement is to be robust. A United Parent Leadership Network began to emerge in 2015 for this purpose in addition to community organizing groups such as the Journey for Justice and the NYC Coalition for Education Justice.

A FINAL THOUGHT

Leadership is an essential asset if our public schools are to succeed and our young people to thrive. From a community school perspective, the leadership of the principal is vital, but leaders from across the community and throughout the school are needed. In today's complex world—a world that has only become more challenging since Gardner first wrote about boundary-crossing leaders in 1993, it is even clearer that no single leader, no single institution can get the results it seeks alone. The movement for community schools is growing. It needs more leaders willing and able to work together for the benefit of our children, our schools, and our democracy.

Chapter Four

Leading through Community-Based Partnerships

Chris Brown

When thinking about leadership in community schools, it is important to consider the role the community can, and should, play in the process of this unique education reform model. Relatively small nonprofit organizations, based in low- and moderate-income communities, have demonstrated real commitment to education change and have been playing a more significant role in school reform. They do this by investing their time, money, and leadership in schools in their community.

The Elev8 program in Chicago is one example of this work. Elev8 is an initiative that grew out of support from the Atlantic Philanthropies for an in-schools integrated services program. In 2006, Atlantic wanted to fund a demonstration program that would marry the best practices in out-of-school-time programming with school-based health services and supports for families. Their goal in this effort was to change the life outcomes of middle school students by addressing their needs, and the needs of their families, in the school space.

Many organizations and people helped lead the Elev8 program from conceptualization through implementation, beginning with Atlantic and its decade-long commitment. Foundation staff conceived of the initial program design, followed by a substantial financial commitment to ensure effective implementation of the program. Administrators and educators at the Chicago Public Schools (CPS) and health care managers and providers from community-based health organizations implemented the program and developed partnerships that improved the lives of young people.

This chapter will focus mainly on the specific leadership role played by nonprofit organizations. This is not to diminish the work of others, but to highlight these important players in the school reform movement whose efforts are often overlooked. The chapter offers lessons on how community organizations can design effective programs, negotiate with funders, schools, and others around issues of interest to the community, and oversee program implementation in a variety of environments. It also shows how these organizations help programs in schools weather the changes that inevitably occur in schools and how they muster political will and local accountability to keep programs in place over which they have a sense of ownership. Lastly, the chapter highlights the importance of long-term commitments by funders to programs and the importance of partnerships at the local school level.

BACKGROUND OF ELEV8

Atlantic selected four sites to implement this program: Baltimore, New Mexico (five schools spread around the state), Oakland, and Chicago. In Chicago, they picked the Local Initiatives Support Corporation (LISC) Chicago to be the intermediary to spearhead the endeavor. For several years, LISC Chicago had been undertaking the New Communities Program (NCP) to support comprehensive community development. It did this by working with a community-based nonprofit lead agency and supporting the development of a quality-of-life plan for the community.

In 2007, LISC selected five of its lead agencies as partners in the Elev8 program. These lead agencies each selected a middle school in their community and, together, they selected a Federally Qualified Health Center (FQHC) as their health provider. LISC facilitated a planning process in each community where 40–120 people came together weekly to plan activities in each of the core program areas.

The lead agencies took responsibility for identifying local leaders who should be a part of the planning. These included staff of the lead agency, principals, teachers, students, parents, social service providers, political leaders, and many others who had a stake in the school. Working with LISC, the lead agencies developed agendas for the meetings, identified key concerns with the effort, led small groups that produced program plans, and worked to develop solutions to problems that arose.

Early in the process, the lead agencies identified three defects in the Elev8 model. Atlantic had a very specific set of "gold standard" out-of-school-time providers they wanted the sites to use for programming. Atlantic originally insisted that the health centers should be run by university-affiliated health providers and that they could only serve students in the school. The last issue that the lead agencies identified was the need for parent, community, and student engagement to be part of the program.

Atlantic wanted to be sure that they were bringing the best options to middle school students and wanted each site to only implement research-based programs in the schools. The lead agencies reacted against this for two reasons. First, many of the providers did not have the capacity to work in more schools in Chicago. Second, and more importantly, the early Elev8 model did not take into account the context of the schools or the communities. What might work or be needed in one place would not work or be needed in another. The LISC planning process allowed local communities and schools to identify their own assets and needs and to design a program around these.

For example, Reavis was a school with a newer principal and a very new teaching staff that had a lot of turnover. Orozco had a principal who had been on the job for more than a decade, as had many of the teachers. Reavis needed its teaching staff to focus on honing their craft. They used Elev8 funds to help with that and brought in outside providers to run the after-school programs. At Orozco, they needed for the teachers to have more time with students outside the formal classroom so they could build deeper relationships with students, so the teachers ran the vast majority of after-school classes. Orozco is also in a predominately Mexican community that is gentrifying and they wanted to run programming that reinforced families' culture.

Local partners quickly identified that using a university-affiliated health provider would have an impact on the long-term sustainability of the health centers. These types of providers do not receive the enhanced reimbursement for Medicaid services that FQHCs do; the vast majority of patients rely on Medicaid for health insurance. LISC subsidized the initial operations of the health center, but lead agencies knew this funding would run out. They had to be sure the health centers could sustain themselves on their own.

The lead agencies also pushed back on the student-only policy, saying it would be hard for them to "sell" the health centers in the community if members of the community were denied access to the center. As one community leader put it, "You want me to tell people in our community (a medically underserved neighborhood) that we are building a state of the art health center in their neighborhood, and they can't use it?" Needless to say, this would not have gone over well. LISC pursued a change in the Chicago zoning code that allowed for an exterior door so that the health centers could see both students and community members

The lead agencies strongly believed that if the program was going to be successful over the long term, the recipients of program services also had to be deeply invested in meaningful ways in the life of the school and the community. Given all the changes that happen in schools, there had to be local political will and accountability that pushed for the program no matter what. To do this, parents, community members, and students had to see themselves as not just passive recipients of services, but as active participants in a vibrant program. Leadership development, arts programming, and educational classes allowed this to happen.

On these points, the local community partners won out. Atlantic agreed that context did matter and allowed local partners to select their own out-of-school-time providers. They agreed to change the model to allow for FQHC providers and for community visits to the health centers. Atlantic also added a fourth pillar to the Elev8 model for parent, community, and student engagement. Today, all of these are recognized as being significant changes and essential elements of the program that helped ensure success over the years.

A successful planning process led to Atlantic Philanthropies providing $18 million in support for implementation in Chicago. At each site, LISC, using funds from Atlantic and other local foundations, provided funding for the lead agency to hire a local program director and other staff, to construct the health centers, to pay for out of school time programs, to provide social supports to students and families, and to hire staff to engage students, parents, and community members in the life of the school.

Today, Elev8 Chicago works in five communities, with five lead agencies, schools, health providers, and other partners (see Table 4.1).

Over the course of the program, each school site has provided fifteen to thirty-five out-of-school-time options per ten-week session and has served over 3,500 students. The health centers have over eight thousand visits per year and have ensured that all five schools have school physical and immunization compliance rates above 95 percent. Over one thousand parents have participated in leadership development, arts, financial, and personal development programming.

Chapin Hall at the University of Chicago is providing the local evaluation for Elev8 Chicago. They have undertaken an implementation evaluation and are in the process of completing an impact evaluation. So far they have seen small but statistically significant improvements in the attendance and behavior of Elev8 participants versus nonparticipants in the same school. They will soon have information comparing students in Elev8 schools to non-Elev8 schools; how well Elev8 participants succeed when they move to high school, and whether use of the health center improves student outcomes.

ADDRESSING CHALLENGES IN IMPLEMENTATION

All of this work has not come without challenges. Perhaps the biggest is the amount of turnover in the school system. Since planning began in 2007, the Chicago Public Schools (CPS) has had six CEOs, the Elev8 schools have had 100 percent principal turnover (in one case the school is on its fifth principal), 50–100 percent turnover of teachers depending on the school, and two

Table 4.1.   Elev8 Community Partnerships

Community	Lead Agency	School	Health Provider
Auburn Gresham	Greater Auburn Gresham Development Corporation (GADC)	Perspectives Calumet Academy	UIC health systems (The health center was originally run by ACCESS Community health, which pulled out in 2014.)
Chicago Lawn	Southwest Organizing Project (SWOP)	Marquette School of Excellence	Esperanza Health Services (The health center was originally run by ACCESS Community health, which pulled out in 2013.)
Kenwood	Quad Communities Development Corporation (QCDC)	Reavis Elementary School	Near North Health Services
Logan Square	Logan Square Neighborhood Association (LSNA)	Ames Middle School (In 2015, LSNA moved the program to McAuliffe and Funston Elementary Schools.)	PrimeCare Health Services
Pilsen	The Resurrection Project (TRP)	Orozco Academy	Alivio Medical Center

schools have been repurposed—one as a turnaround with Academy for School Leadership (AUSL) and another converted into a military academy, and because of the nature of the program, a complete turnover of the student body twice.

Given this, someone has to provide stability if the program is going to be successful. The community-based lead agencies play this role. During this same period, there has been no change in the executive directors of the five lead agencies. Four of the five Elev8 directors have only turned over once, and the other one has turned over three times. In three of these five cases, the previous director took another position within the organization and is still connected with the program.

Through their stability, the lead agencies provide leadership to the education efforts in the school. They have built lasting relationships with parents and students that transcend turnover at the schools. Often, students are looking for Elev8 staff when the school year starts because they don't know any of the school staff. The Elev8 staff helps them weather the stormy period that often happens when new teachers and principals take over a school.

The lead agencies also have provided the political will and accountability to keep the program going in a way that an inside-the-system person or an outside-the-community organization could not. Because these organizations are deeply rooted in their community they have lots of political capital they can use to implement their will. Often when a new principal comes in to a school, they have their ideas about what can and should be done in the building. While the groups do not presume to tell them how to run the academic program of the school, they do remind them of commitments and investments made in the community school program of Elev8.

In each of the cases above when turnover happened, Elev8 could have been lost at the school. This happened in schools in Elev8 New Mexico. A new principal came in, wanted to move the school in a different direction, and booted out the Elev8 program. There was no on-the-ground community partner there to ensure a successful transition of the program. In Chicago, in each case where a new principal has transitioned into a school, the Elev8 community-based lead agency was there to help them with their transition and to also ensure that the program stayed in place and continued to deliver services and programming much as it had in the past.

Another key challenge that the lead agencies addressed was the siloed nature of schoolwork and social service delivery. Principals are evaluated on improving test scores. Health center directors are judged on how many patients they saw and after-school providers on how many children attend their program. While they may all agree that working together is in their best long-term interest, it is hard to do this when there are so many short-term pressures.

STRUCTURING COMMUNITY COLLABORATION

The lead agencies provide both the space and the time as well as the political cover to allow for collaboration. The lead agencies all have relationships that go beyond just the school building. They know the principal's boss and the CEO of the FQHC. The lead agencies and/or LISC have relationships with school board members and senior leaders at CPS. At times when the principals feel pressed, the lead agency can open up space for them to work on Elev8. The reverse is also true in that the executive directors at times have used their relationships with others to get the principals to pay attention to Elev8 when they have drifted to other issues.

LISC Chicago often describes the lead agencies as the glue that holds the Elev8 program together in the school. The Elev8 director is the one person in the school who is paid to get people to work together and whose evaluation is based on how well they do this. The directors convene meetings, monthly or quarterly, with academic staff, health providers, after-school providers, and others to be sure that everyone is working together on Elev8 goals. They use these meetings to identify and solve problems, make long-term plans for collaboration, and follow through on implementation to the benefit of students.

The current academic performance measures also provide a challenge. Everyone knows that arts, sports, cooking, gardening, and a whole wide range of other programs are important to build well-rounded students. But because of budget cuts and a focus on accountability measures that only look at reading and math test scores, many of the enrichment programs that richer school districts offer are not available in the Elev8 schools. The community groups led the way in insisting that the kids in these schools have options that go beyond just basic education.

The Elev8 program provided the funding to make up for budget cuts. The lead agencies pushed to ensure that the schools looked at other measures of success. These included demonstrating competency in the arts. After each ten-week session, the Elev8 program organized a showcase where students could show off what they learned in their classes. This was also a great way to bring parents, community members, and others into the school building.

The lead agencies also promoted social emotional learning. Depending on the school, they did this with peace circles, peer juries, calm classroom practices, and group and individual counseling sessions.

The Elev8 program offered lots of opportunities to learn about keys to success of a community school program. These relate to relationship building by the lead agency, integration of the work, and the staffing of the program.

As with many things in life, community schools often were about *who* you know, not *what* you know. The community-based lead agencies were very effective in building relationships and partnerships with a wide variety of people and organizations to implement the Elev8 program. They worked closely with principals and leaders of the FQHCs to identify shared interests and then to act on that knowledge. They were very good at bringing in outside partners and helping them navigate the school system—getting security background checks, understanding the school day schedule, and getting paid. They also developed strong and deep relationships with students and families, often around noneducational or school issues, that allowed them to understand what families needed, but also what they had to offer the program. School staff could not have done this because they did not have the staff or the time to do this relationship building.

Because they had these relationships with all these different partners, the lead agencies were able to promote the integration of programs. Since the lead agencies were not pressed by short-term concerns such as annual test score increases or patient visit requirements, they were able to focus on longer-term goals for students' development. The lead agencies acted as the glue holding the Elev8 program together at the local level. They convened meetings, collected and disseminated data, identified roadblocks and solutions, cajoled and pushed partners some times and provided political cover for staff when needed at other times, and consistently reconnected people to the plan they had made and agreed to.

The program provided for a number of staff people to help carry out this work. A key agreement early on was that most of the staff, and the program director in particular, would be employees of the lead agency. While they were housed at the school and worked closely with school staff, they answered to the executive director of the community partner, rather than the principal. While the principal was a key player in the implementation of the program, everyone realized that schools are chronically understaffed and that any additional staff, such as an Elev8 program director, would be moved around to plug holes in the school staffing plan. By having the director and their staff report to the lead agency, they could avoid having staff "drift" from the program.

Marquette School of Excellence offers a good case study in how all this community leadership played out. Marquette is located in the Chicago Lawn community on Chicago's southwest side. The school is a large one and almost exactly half African American and half Latino. The Southwest Organizing Project selected Marquette in 2007 as their Elev8 partner. It had been one of three original community schools in Chicago funded by the Polk Bros. Foundation and Metropolitan Family Services (MFS) was still working in the school, mostly with younger children. Elev8 offered an opportunity to bring more programing to the older students and their families.

SWOP led a planning process at the school in 2007 that included about 120 people; from the principal and teachers to students and parents to local service organizations and MFS. The program began implementation in 2008 and was focused on converting the middle grades program into an International Baccalaureate curriculum with a strong, supporting after-school component.

While the program did good work and provided needed services and opportunities to students and families, it was not enough to turn around the academic performance of the school. In 2012, Marquette was targeted for turnaround, meaning all the teachers would be released and a new administration would be brought in. At about the same time, ACCESS, the FQHC health provider, announced that it would be leaving the school. In most cases, this would have been the end of the community school program as a new administration coming in under these circumstances would want all "new" things in the building.

SWOP stepped in though and worked closely with AUSL even before it came to the school to help AUSL build connections with local parents and help them understand the turnaround process and to convince AUSL that Elev8 was an important program to the community that needed to be left in place during the turnaround process.

SWOP also worked to bring in a new FQHC partner to run the health center. SWOP identified and recruited Esperanza, an FQHC from Chicago's Little Village community, to come and run the health center at the school.

As all these new organizations settled into the school, SWOP staff, who were in place before the changes, brought partners together to build relationships and create new plans for Elev8's work at the school. Today, Elev8 and all the partners—AUSL, Esperanza, and SWOP—are fully integrated into the life of the school and into each other's work. They meet regularly to plan programs and to target which students most need Elev8 services. They combine funding to pay for behavioral health services. They jointly fund-raise for other school needs. In many ways, they have a much stronger partnership for the Elev8 program than existed before all the transitions. This was all due to SWOP's leadership in bringing them together.

CONCLUDING THOUGHTS

Community schools help to integrate schools into the life of a community and vice versa. They create learning opportunities for students and families that are often not available in many schools. They provide resources to school staff and leaders that they might not otherwise have access to. They break down common barriers to education in low- and moderate-income communities.

As the name implies, though, the community must be a big part of community schools if they are to be successful. Elev8 Chicago offers many examples of how community-based lead agencies have played a key role in ensuring the success of these schools. The lead agencies provided leadership in the planning and implementation of the program, they kept the effort going with staff and additional resources, they built partnerships and problem solved, and they held the effort to together when the winds of change could have easily blown the effort apart.

Chapter Five

Academic Achievement and the Community Schools Model

Mary A. Ronan

From the beginning, Community Schools—or Community Learning Centers, as they are known in Cincinnati—were rooted in the imperative of improving educational outcomes for students. They were about many other important values as well: reconnecting schools to the communities they serve, overcoming the health and social-emotional barriers confronting many families, and providing recreational and arts enrichment opportunities that heighten the vibrancy of family experiences and neighborhood life. In Cincinnati, Community Learning Centers also were the means of fulfilling a promise that was made to voters when Cincinnati Public Schools sought local funding for what became a $1 billion Facilities Master Plan to rebuild or fully renovate schools for every student. These upgraded schools, taxpayers were told, would be about more than bricks and mortar; they also would restore schools as centers of community. Voters responded and, in 2003, the bond issue was approved.

Yet, the "learning" component of Cincinnati's Community Learning Centers, by necessity, never wavered. As academic standards and state accountability measures changed, and as district improvement strategies were refocused in response, our Community Learning Centers (CLCs) have evolved to become better aligned with academic goals and to leverage the resources of partners more effectively.

Any effective superintendent of an urban school system with diverse demographics and complex needs quickly learns that to try to go it alone would be folly. Fortunately, with Community Learning Centers and the policies and practices that support them, a succession of superintendents and boards of education in Cincinnati hasn't been required to address the needs of families and neighborhoods in isolation. Instead, the story of our Community Learning Centers has been a story of a community and a school district coming together in mutual commitment to support the success of its children, its schools, and its neighborhoods.

SEEDS OF CINCINNATI'S CLCS

The concept of partners contributing to school success is not new. As in many city school districts across the country, even in the late twentieth century, when urban schools were generally perceived to be disconnected from the neighborhoods they served, community participation never completely waned in Cincinnati. Community members, agencies, and local businesses still were showing up, offering to tutor, mentor, or donate supplies and to provide some health services or career training. While these efforts were well-meaning, there was no real evidence that they were helping students and schools to succeed.

Inspired by the leadership of the late Ohio Gov. John Gilligan, a member of the Cincinnati Board of Education at the time and a champion of the community schools concept, the Cincinnati school board laid the groundwork for tighter alignment with academic goals in the late 1990s and early 2000s. In 2001, the board approved Guiding Principles for Community Learning Centers, which set the expectation that schools and communities collaborate "to set expectations, foster diversity, and share accountability for results." Further, the guiding principles stated that schools should use their district-required academic improvement plans to "develop the partnerships needed to enhance opportunities for student success and community investment." The principles also specified that, where the school and community deem it appropriate, partner organizers and staff may locate in the schools to deliver services.

At about this same time, Cincinnati Public Schools was gearing up for a massive school rebuilding plan. A 1996 federal General Accounting Office report had concluded that Ohio had the worst public school buildings in the nation, and Cincinnati's schools were among the oldest and most deteriorated in the state. A Facilities Master Plan adopted by the district in 2002, to be funded partially by the state but mostly with local revenue, outlined plans to provide first-class school buildings while eliminating excess space created through years of declining enrollment. This meant that some schools would close—never a popular proposition—but with the pledge that all students would have better facilities when the building program was completed.

THE POWER OF ENGAGEMENT

Following the approval of a bond issue for the local share of funding for the Facilities Master Plan in spring of 2003, Cincinnati Public Schools set about fulfilling the promise of creating Community Learning Centers that would transform schools and revitalize communities. A community engagement campaign, led by the Children's Defense Fund and the KnowledgeWorks Foundation, was launched in the city's fifty-two neighborhoods as well as in surrounding municipalities included in the district's boundaries. Following these outreach efforts, Cincinnati Public Schools and the Children's Defense Fund developed written plans for community engagement in developing Community Learning Centers. These plans introduced the role of a resource coordinator—whose job would be to cultivate partnerships in response to specific school and neighborhood needs—as a linchpin of each Community Learning Center.

As a proud "city of neighborhoods," it was understood in Cincinnati that the needs and priorities of each school and community it served would vary. Just as school and community representatives were involved as members of every school's building design team, so were they part of the development of every school's Community Learning Center. Neither took a "cookie cutter" approach in analyzing and responding to school and neighborhood expectations and visions for success.

Partnerships were developed in response to identified needs—and in conjunction with the building planning—were provided space in the new or renovated school facilities. Two of the earliest buildings and Community Learning Centers to open under the Facilities Master Plan were examples of the synergy of this engagement process. Rockdale Academy opened in January 2005 with a 1,200-square-foot health clinic built into the new school. Riverview East Academy opened the following year with a child care provider, Cincinnati Early Learning Centers, built into the school design.

At the same time, as the engagement experience grew and more school buildings came on line, it became apparent that while each Community Learning Center was unique, common needs were emerging for many schools. In response, like agencies began working together to create a system of matching specific services to specific schools. For example, Mindpeace became the partnership network for behavioral health services and Growing Well Cincinnati became the network for general health services and support. Other agencies began to meet together to look at data and common practice. Resource Coordinators worked with these networks to identify partnerships and expand services. Witnessing the power of the Community Learning Centers model unfold, the Cincinnati Board of Education adopted a policy declaring that, over time, every school in the district would be a Community Learning Center and that each CLC would have a resource coordinator.

WHAT GETS MEASURED . . .

In Cincinnati Public Schools, a pilot project to place resource coordinators at nine Community Learning Centers initially was funded through several 21st Century Community Learning Center grants for academic enrichment programs. The Greater Cincinnati Foundation and United Way of Cincinnati invested $1 million over five years in the initiative. Later the district contributed Title I funding to support the resource coordinators, and a few lead agencies—including Cincinnati Community Learning Centers Institute and Families Forward—paid for the resource coordinators in the schools they served.

As CLCs took root and gained community support, the state of Ohio began to issue the first iterations in a series of school and district report cards. By the late 2000s, twenty-six district schools were designated as Community Learning Centers. Unfortunately, some of them had been designated as in Academic Emergency from the inception of the state's report card ratings.

This caused Cincinnati Public Schools and our partners to take an unblinking look at the impact of Community Learning Centers on academic achievement and ask hard—but necessary—questions:

- How is investment in CLCs impacting student achievement?
- What does success look like, and how do we get there?

In response, a data-informed process was introduced, designed to measure results and prescribe corresponding actions. Sixteen elementary schools with low academic ratings engaged in a pilot project using the new process and tracking the results of individual students responding to CLC services. The pilot highlighted the importance of intense use of data to drive decisions and track results.

Resource coordinators in this pilot were challenged to take on a stronger analytic role to foster accountability throughout the system. Working with principals and partners, they used both academic and nonacademic data to allocate partner resources, monitor results, and minimize barriers to academic achievement.

A powerful tool in harnessing data from the CLCs in the pilot was the Learning Partner Dashboard, a digital data-management system designed by Cincinnati Public Schools in partnership with Strive (a collaborative educational network that began in Cincinnati), Microsoft, and Procter & Gamble for the purpose of tracking individual student progress. This electronic tool replaced mountains of spreadsheets formerly used by resource coordinators to try to gauge the effectiveness of partner strategies to improve student success. The pilot yielded promising practices connected to improved academic results, later validated in an independent evaluation by Cincinnati

Children's Hospital Medical Center's Innovations section. In 2010, when new state ratings were announced, thirteen of the sixteen low-performing pilot schools experienced measurable improvement, with five jumping two full categories in the state ratings. Cincinnati Public Schools simultaneously became the first urban district in Ohio to earn an Effective rating on the State Report Card.

SUSTAINING SUCCESS

The pilot's success demonstrated the value of using data as a lever for academic success and led to a desire to ensure that the approach is used to engender continuous improvement in all of our district's Community Learning Centers, which, at this writing, number forty-two of fifty-five total schools.

A model called REFORM was created to guide successful resource coordination. Reform is an acronym for the steps in the process:

- *R*eview data and set goals
- *E*ngage partners
- *F*ocus on individual students
- *O*ffer support
- *R*eset
- *M*easure Impact

The notion of steps actually is a misnomer because the process is not consecutive; rather, the components overlap as part of an ongoing process that requires continual review and management.

R = Review Data and Set Goals

Data are the starting point for homing in on a school's trends and challenges, deciding what resources are needed to impact school success, and establishing partner goals in response. The trends can be both academic and non-academic—for example, too many third graders not reading on grade level, or a high incidence of a health trend like asthma or childhood obesity.

In Cincinnati, the resource coordinator and the school principal together review the data collected by the resource coordinator and prepare a preliminary evaluation of needs and trends. The data sources are summarized in Table 5.1.

Once preliminary data have been reviewed by the principal and the resource coordinator, a data review team is assembled. Key stakeholders on the team typically include the principal; school governance committee member or chairperson; teachers, school instructional management team members

Table 5.1.   Objective and Subjective Data Sources for Review

	Academic	*Health & Wellness*	*Partner*	*Parent*	*Community*
Objective	State test data from previous year and current pretest; attendance data, discipline data, college placement data.	Numbers of health screenings, visual, dental, and mental health contacts.	Number of students participating in activities; Learning Partner Dashboard progress data.	Parent attendance at conferences and events; parent demographic data; number of parents accessing electronic academic data on students.	Number of community members involved in the school; community demographics, number of business partners.
Subjective	School culture, barriers to learning.	Health, literacy, cultural influences, family, and diet habits.	Partner satisfaction, anecdotal reports by students, parents.	Communication with parents, parental interests.	Community relationships, school's reputation in the community.

and academic coaches; health professionals, such as the school nurse; a representative of the school's lead agency; and a community leader, such as the president of the neighborhood council. The data review team analyzes trends and sets specific, measurable goals and meets throughout the school year to look at new data and assess progress toward goals.

E = Engage Partners

Securing the right partners to meet the Community Learning Center's goals is critically important. In Cincinnati, the resource coordinator leads and facilitates all aspects of partner engagement, from identifying and successfully recruiting partners, to integrating them into the school, to nurturing partner relationships, to supporting each partner's ability to get positive results.

The underpinning of effective partner engagement is a broad knowledge of the community's issues, strengths, and assets, which then can be tapped to meet a Community Learning Center's goals. The process begins with the resource coordinator conducting a gap analysis identifying unmet needs and clarifying the partners who should be engaged. Once recruited, partners are introduced to school staff and culture through orientation sessions, and individual volunteers are provided with information on district policies, background checks and security badges.

Resource coordinators establish both formal and informal agreements with partners. Formal agreements include a signed memorandum of understanding that includes a statement of goals, how they are aligned with school needs, and expected outcomes. These signed agreements are requirements for all partners proving ongoing services or activities at the Community Learning Center and signal agreement on policies.

F = Focus on Individual Students

While there is collective benefit to a school from Community Learning Centers partnerships, the impact is most powerful when partner services are tailored to the students who need them most. In Cincinnati, the electronic data-focused Learning Partner Dashboard helps Resource Coordinators identify these students and monitor their progress.

Targeting individual students as priorities for services does not mean abandoning other students at the Community Learning Center. Rather, a targeted approach narrows and intensifies the focus while making it possible to assess the effectiveness of resource coordination. At most Community Learning Centers in Cincinnati Public Schools, at least 125 students are targeted for CLC services or programs. They are identified based on an analysis that they will help meet CLC goals if gains are experienced.

For example, a high school wishing to increase its attendance rate to 92 percent is able to use the data dashboard to identify the students most likely to fall short of the goal and target them for services. On the flip side, students with high attendance averages can be identified as potential peer mentors.

Resource Coordinators track the number of targeted students being served by partners, with the goal of serving 100 percent of them, then monitor the outcomes for those students. Independent evaluations have demonstrated that academic achievement increases for students targeted for services through the Community Learning Centers model in Cincinnati.

O = Offer Support

Providing opportunities for ongoing partner support, we've discovered, is one of the most important components of successful Community Learning Centers. Even the most effective partner organizations have room to grow, and the dynamic of K–12 public education in this nation seems in a perpetual state of change. New standards, testing, and accountability systems roll out, often with little notice. District improvement strategies priorities are tweaked to deliver on new state and federal mandates. Information and training are vital for partners and resource coordinators alike to stay up to date and marshal resources to meet evolving demands. In Cincinnati, this support is offered at both the school and district levels.

Partner meetings at schools provide a platform for sharing school successes and challenges, promoting open communication, and deepening the relationship between the school and its partners. Student data are shared in aggregate (so as not to violate student privacy), and partners who have completed a district student data-sharing permission form may directly monitor progress of students accessing their services. The Resource Coordinator schedules monthly meetings and prepares meaningful agendas to guide meaty discussions and productive outcomes. Frequently principals attend these meetings to share updates on school progress and thank partners for their contributions.

Expressing appreciation cannot be overlooked as means of partner support. Too often, in the press of school life (and, regrettably, sometimes in life outside of school) we miss opportunities to celebrate accomplishments with a simple "thank you." Resource Coordinators provide such occasions through Partner Appreciation Days, newsletters that highlight partners' impact on the school and neighborhood, and certificates of appreciation or cards from students.

R = Reset

Continual monitoring of student data almost always leads, sooner or later, to a reset of partner strategies. On a district level, a major reset occurred in 2010, when our Elementary Initiative was introduced to focus on sixteen low-achieving elementary schools that had languished as poor performers for several years. A set of targeted strategies was put into place along with resources to support them, and the vast majority of these schools improved academically.

Similarly, reset at the school level doesn't occur haphazardly. Data drive the assessment, the decision, and the action calculated to achieve the greatest impact. For example, a student may appear to be successfully engaged in tutoring while data show that the student is not gaining skills in the targeted tutoring area. A closer look may reveal that the tutor is not using materials correctly, and additional tutor training or a switch in tutors may be necessary.

Every January, a formal reset process is scheduled to analyze results to date, which by then include two student report cards and some preliminary state testing data. Data for all students are reviewed and services are adjusted accordingly.

Occasionally, the reset leads to the conclusion that the partner organization needs intervention and additional training and support to function effectively. In rare cases—and only after efforts have been made to improve partner success—a partner may be asked to terminate services if they are of poor quality and not in the best interest of students. This decision is made by the principal and the school's governance committee.

M = Measure Impact

At the end of every school year, an intensive analysis of all Community Learning Centers data is conducted by an independent, external evaluator. This is the moment of truth for resource coordination in Cincinnati's CLCs. It's how we are able to prove that these centers are fulfilling their promise of school and community transformation and thus are worthy of continued investment. Funders and supporters—including our own Board of Education members—expect no less.

This analysis informs the data review that occurs at the beginning of next school year as the results from the prior year are assessed against the bold, specific, and measurable goals that were set. The ultimate question: Did a school's Community Learning Center partnerships make a difference in meeting the goals? Results are widely shared with stakeholders and successes celebrated.

By measuring impact and ensuring transparency through third-party analysis, we progress from assumptions and opinions to being able to confidently affirm how integrating partnership services into educational goals is making a difference for students, families, schools, and communities.

THE TEST OF TIME

Community Learning Centers partnerships have been a feature of every major successful academic initiative in Cincinnati Public Schools since I assumed the role of superintendent (initially on an interim basis) in August 2008. The early pilot of resource coordinators using a data-informed model to provide targeted partner support coincided with the introduction of the Elementary Initiative and strengthened the external resources working to lift student achievement in sixteen low-performing elementary schools. The result was significant—substantial in several instances—academic growth in most of those schools, leading to Cincinnati Public Schools becoming the first urban school system in Ohio to achieve an Effective rating on the State Report Card, a feat repeated the following year.

As the state changed accountability systems and report card measures, tracking "apples-to-apples" progress over time has become more challenging. But in terms of one state measure that has remained constant, Cincinnati Public Schools remains the top-performing urban school system in a state in which eight big-city school systems vie for that distinction. Our district continues to lead peer school systems in the Performance Index, a calculation of student performance on all state tests in all content areas at all tested grades and performance levels. Community Learning Centers also have demonstrated the flexibility to respond effectively to new state mandates and district initiatives designed to deliver upon them.

In 2013, Ohio Gov. John Kasich persuaded the Ohio Legislature to enact into law the Third Grade Guarantee, a high-stakes mandate that required that students who did not read on grade level by the end of third grade not be promoted in reading to the fourth grade. In response, partner resources in Community Learning Centers—especially tutors—focused on assisting struggling primary grade students in mastering early literacy skills. Results were impressive: At the beginning of the 2014–15 school year, 97 percent of Cincinnati Public Schools' third graders had met the standards for promotion into the fourth grade based on reading proficiency scores, a rate that exceeded the state average. The following year, the rate increased to 98 percent, despite the state's increasing the "cut score" for reading grade-level proficiency.

At the beginning of the 2014–15 school year, our district began a phased implementation of the My Tomorrow initiative, initially focused on seventh and eighth graders and designed to ensure that 100 percent of Cincinnati Public Schools' seventh graders graduate not only on-time, but also fully prepared to implement their chosen paths for college and careers. In the 2015–16 school year, the initiative expanded to fully include grades seven through twelve (all high schools in Cincinnati Public Schools now comprise grades seven through twelve), with a mentoring and career exploration component known as "advisory" extending to fifth and sixth grades.

Again, Community Learning Center partnerships have been central to this work. A new partnership supported by business representatives and the Cincinnati USA Regional Chamber of Commerce—The Business-Education Connectivity Council—was created to help students explore and better prepare for career areas, potentially addressing the job gaps that exist in our region. Other partners have stepped in to contribute to additional focus areas of the initiative: college access, real-world connections, proficiency in technology and software, mentoring, and development of leadership skills.

Even as we work to refine best practices and recognize the potential to improve, Cincinnati's Community Learning Centers continue to receive recognition as an outstanding model of school reform by the Coalition of Community Schools, the American Federation of Teachers and the U.S. Department of Education. While appreciative, we understand there is another dimension to the success of our collective partnerships: their impact on individuals.

FACES OF CLCS

While vitally important and essential for accountability, data don't tell the entire story of Community Learning Centers in Cincinnati. Behind every statistic are real children, families, and community members whose lives are better because of CLCs and the partnerships that support them. Meet three of them:

Sadie

Sadie was a second grader at Oyler School with a winning personality and long, carrot-colored hair when her tutor noticed a problem: As Sadie struggled to complete math problems, her numbers were running off the page. Suspecting that Sadie might have trouble seeing, she was referred to the new OneSight Vision Center at Oyler School, a first-of-its-kind, school-based comprehensive vision center that continues to provide eye exams, vision services, and glasses to students throughout the district. It turned out that Sadie was seven times more farsighted than normal. Within days, Sadie was fitted for glasses and got to choose her own frames. "I picked them because they are pretty and pink," she said. With corrected vision, her schoolwork improved and her confidence soared.

Nhy'aire

Thanks to help from tutors at Hays-Porter School's Community Learning Center, Nhy'aire overcame his struggles in primary grades developing early literacy skills to become an avid, proficient reader. In fact, Nhy'aire earned his school's highest score on the Ohio Achievement Test in reading in 2014. "When reading was hard, it was kind of stressful," Nhy'aire said. "They pushed me to work hard. And then, the light came on and I could read! I was happy and excited." Nhy'aire, who loves the library, checks out a variety of books every day. Partial to books about animals, he has set his sights on becoming a veterinarian.

Zaire

A partnership with GE Aviation at her elementary school, Evanston Academy, inspired Zaire to get excited about science and a career as a computer scientist. Zaire and her Evanston Academy teammates swept the 2013–14 middle school robotics competition, capturing seven of eight first-place trophies. At the same time, the students helped pilot a partnership involving GE Aviation and the Smithsonian's National Air and Space Museum. "In science class, we got to Skype with the Smithsonian," she said. "We talked about the Mars Rover, and compared it to our robot and how it was programmed. I like science, math, and computers. I want to work in 'hard' math." Now in high school, Zaire credits the GE-Smithsonian partnerships for helping to prepare her for increasingly complex science and math concepts.

CONCLUDING THOUGHTS

The success and durability of Community Learning Centers in Cincinnati are a testament to the many individuals, partner organizations, funders, resource coordinators and school and district employees who believe in their power to transform schools and revitalize communities. Our school system and our community owe much to their shared passion, hard work, and commitment to continually learn and grow. This chapter would not be possible without their contributions, leading to the best practices described in Cincinnati Public Schools' Community Learning Centers Manual for resource coordinators, from whose wisdom I have liberally (and, at times, literally) borrowed in this text.

Chapter Six

The Rural Solution: How Community Schools Can Reinvigorate Rural Education

Dorris Terry Williams[1]

One in five students in the United States—19.4 percent—attends a public elementary or secondary school designated as rural. The view outside the classroom window for some of these students is "one of scenic fields, pasture lands, or forests nestled at the base of mountains" (Shamah & MacTavish, 2009, p. 1). But variations across rural America can be stunning. Some students have a view of the polluted coastline where their parents, grandparents, and even great grandparents used to make a living, the abandoned mining equipment that once tied their families' livelihoods to the company store, or the vast clear-cut space that was once a forest amid rolling hills. These visual contrasts mirror the diverse cultural, social, economic, and political realities that make rural places what they are today.

The situations surrounding rural education—like the views from the classroom windows—vary widely from place to place. But what rural places have in common is the challenge to provide a quality education to ensure the success of some 10 million students. This challenge often comes with difficult odds—inadequate financing, teacher shortages, and inaccessible or unaffordable services for children and families. The partnerships and approach of "full-service community schools" may hold the greatest potential for addressing rural education's challenges and ensuring that every child has at least a near-equal opportunity to succeed.

This chapter examines community schools from a rural perspective. It provides a context for rural community schools and discusses the need for clarification of the language used to describe the concept of community school. Three examples of successful rural community schools provide a framework for discussing the benefits, characteristics, and policy implications of rural community schools.

In particular, this chapter addresses some of the challenges that rural areas confront in attempting to implement a community school strategy and offers recommendations for overcoming them.

States and rural districts should develop a rural teacher recruitment strategy that emphasizes the benefits of teaching in a community school. An important aspect of state rural recruitment strategies could be permitting local school boards to implement community educator certification programs. This would allow school districts to place highly skilled and knowledgeable community members in classrooms under the supervision of highly qualified, highly effective teachers of record. This type of program can facilitate the movement of parent and community volunteers into the teaching profession in understaffed areas, particularly when combined with emerging "grow-your-own" teacher recruitment and retention strategies.

Rural schools and districts should remove barriers to substantive parental and community engagement in schools. Districts and schools can develop programs and services that bring adults into the school building both as consumers and as volunteers, and they can revise policies that discourage parent and community engagement. Schools should partner with community-based, nongovernmental organizations to provide alternative venues for parents and community members to participate in decision-making and interact with children in academic and nonacademic contexts.

New school planning should incorporate multiple related community needs. Local governments should consider bringing together schools and child and family services under the same roof before deciding to build new structures or otherwise providing separate housing for schools and services. States should harmonize construction standards by categorical funding sources when it does not compromise the public purpose served by the standards.

States should help to reduce financial risk to community school partners when they undertake new construction projects. State legislatures should create and administer a joint-use-guarantee fund that insures against loss of fiscal capacity to meet bond payments when a partner is forced to abandon the joint-use facilities before the terms of the financing are fulfilled due to state or local government action. Legislatures should also create a Rural Joint Use Public Facilities Commission to identify statutory and administrative barriers to joint-use facilities and recommend policy changes specific to their respective states.

Congress and state legislatures should provide incentives for, and place special emphasis on, the explicit development and implementation of community schools as a turnaround strategy for high-needs and low-performing schools in rural areas. Community schools are a promising alternative strategy for these schools in rural areas, yet the necessary resources are not available from the 2015 Every Student Succeeds Act.

Congress and state legislatures should increase investments in community schools. State governments should fund strategic planning processes for community school development and implementation in rural places, the federal government should increase funding for the Full Service Community Schools Program, and the U.S. Department of Education should provide technical assistance through intermediary organizations to help level the field for rural districts in competitive grant competitions.

Full-service community schools may well provide the greatest opportunity for quality education and success in rural communities where resources are few. Community schools offer a much-needed alternative to traditional schooling models even in rural communities that are not economically stressed.

ISSUES FACING RURAL SCHOOLS

Rural schools are expected to provide a quality education for all students while overcoming challenges such as transportation barriers, strained resources, and lack of access to needed services. Yet these schools are most often at the mercy of others who are external to the school system to provide them with the means to accomplish that goal. School districts depend primarily upon funding made available by local, state, and federal policy makers. The ability to attract and retain effective teachers, provide and maintain suitable facilities, and have children enter school ready to learn are all issues that extend beyond the school itself. These issues take on particular significance in rural areas, and all sectors of the community and all levels of government must see them as a shared responsibility.

Finding the Will to Educate

The history of race, power, and oppression in the United States, combined with the disadvantages suffered disproportionately by children of color and children of poverty, suggests that providing a quality education for all children may be as much a matter of political will as it is a matter of resources in many rural communities. The problem is especially prevalent in the rural South, where the high number and percentage of rural children of color lead many to believe that the quality of education is a manifestation of systematic, institutionalized oppression (Williams & Johnson, 2002).

The National Algebra Project, founded by distinguished scholar and Civil Rights icon Bob Moses, has compared the current crisis in the education of poor children and children of color to the systematically contrived illiteracy of sharecroppers who were denied an education and subsequently denied the right to vote because of their illiteracy. "Sharecropper illiteracy," the organ-ization stated in a memorandum to participants in its first national conference on quality education, "was the hidden subtext of the struggle for the right to vote and the systematic denial of the opportunity for a quality public school education has been the hidden subtext of the struggle for political rights in the broadest sense in this country" (Algebra Project, Inc., 2005). The history of Native American education in the United States raises similar concerns.

Attracting and Retaining Effective Teachers

Schools across the country struggle to attract and retain effective teachers. Many rural schools face the unique challenge of trying to attract teachers to high-needs, low-amenity areas while being unable to pay salaries competi-tive with suburban and urban schools. Rural schools are often forced to take drastic measures to overcome teacher shortages including consolidating classes, employing out-of-field teachers, and decreasing course offerings (Ji-merson, 2003).

Addressing Students' Special Needs

Rural students face many of the same difficulties as urban students in receiv-ing much-needed health and social services. The low number of health care providers in rural areas limits access to medical, mental health, and dental care (Southwest Rural Health Research Center, 2010). Distance and limited transportation options may make it difficult for families to tap into services that might be provided by informal associations and organizations, as well as the more formal social service providers such as county welfare offices, public health services, and food distribution centers.

Providing Access to Community Institutions

Many rural students spend two hours or more a day getting to and from school. The time required to go to and from school can reduce opportunities for students to engage in extracurricular and after-school enrichment activ-ities. Students may also travel from areas where access to community institu-tions such as libraries, parks, recreation centers, and theaters is limited or nonexistent.

Maintaining Public Facilities

Many rural communities need new or upgraded public facilities, including new school buildings, but funding new construction and upgrading existing structures is a persistent challenge (Dewees, 1999). Rural school districts especially suffer when school construction allocations are tied to property values since they tend to have lower property value assessments. Older rural residents who live in higher-value property areas and do not have school-aged children may be unwilling to pay for necessary improvements. And rural communities may find it difficult to galvanize support for bond issues, further complicating a district's ability to build new facilities (Dewees, 1999; Stern, 1994).

THE COMMUNITY SCHOOL SOLUTION

Full-service community schools are potentially an important solution to the problems confronting many rural children, families, and schools today. That can include the issues of inequity in services and of social, economic, and political injustice. Indeed, community schools hold perhaps the greatest potential of all innovations to fulfill our responsibility as a democratic society to provide a quality education for all children. The community school model can capitalize on many of the assets offered in rural schools.

Unfortunately, the community school concept is couched in language that has become so polluted that the concept sometimes gets distorted, and the language becomes a tool for promoting ill-intentioned agendas. "Neighborhood schools," "community schools," and "good schools close to home" can all become codes for the resegregation of schools, most often on the basis of race but also on the basis of socioeconomics. There must be a broader and more justice-oriented understanding of the concept of "community" in order for the concept of community schools to be useful in high-needs, racially and ethnically heterogeneous settings. This is not to suggest that schools that are racially, ethnically, or socioeconomically distinct cannot be good community schools. It is a reminder, however, that community is not merely a geographically defined space where groups of people live with institutions and structures that serve their common interests. Community is also a place where people and institutions, including schools, collaborate to build social capital that in turn strengthens schools, families, and communities.

Author Peter Block emphasizes that the term "community" insinuates both ownership and membership. Community, he says, "is about the experience of belonging. . . . To belong to a community is to act as a creator or co-owner of that community. . . . Community is the container within which our longing to be is fulfilled" (Block, 2009, p. xii). What, then, is a community school? The U.S. Department of Education defines a full-service community school as an "elementary or secondary school that works with its local educational agency and community-based organizations, nonprofit organizations, and other public or private entities to provide a coordinated and integrated set of comprehensive academic, social, and health services that respond to the needs of its students, students' family members, and community members."

The school's "results-focused partnerships . . . are based on identified needs and organized around a set of mutually defined results and outcomes" (Federal Register, 2010, p. 6188).

The Coalition for Community Schools defines a community school as "both a place and a set of partnerships between the school and other community resources. Its integrated focus on academics, health and social services, youth and community development, and community engagement leads to improved student learning, stronger families, and healthier communities. Schools become centers of the community and are open to everyone—all day, every day, evenings and weekends" (Coalition for Community Schools, n.d.).

How then can we operationalize these notions of community schools in rural areas? Engagement in community schools occurs when parents, students, school staff, and neighbors invest in the school, co-creating and owning it. There is a conscious effort to ensure that services are not merely co-located but integrated in a way that increases the social capital that goes into overcoming or removing the barriers to student, family, and community success and citizenship.

A focus on community building allows these schools to become centers that practice the basic principles of a democratic society and remove the sense of isolation, and where "service providers" see themselves and are seen as community members guided by those same principles. This deeper sense of community may make community schools unrivaled in their potential to provide quality education for all children, whether urban or rural. A commitment to the principles implied by this broader understanding of community is an opportunity to change the discourse and direction of education in rural areas. It provides an opportunity to confront the issues of race, power, and injustice that have obstructed the success of children and families and threatened the security of our nation as a whole.

THREE EXAMPLES OF EFFECTIVE
RURAL COMMUNITY SCHOOLS

The following are three examples of effective rural community schools: Owsley Elementary School in Booneville, Kentucky; Molly Stark School in Bennington, Vermont; and Noble High School in North Berwick, Maine. These cases provide guidance and encouragement for low-resource, rural communities that often succumb to poverty and isolation and accept less than they would hope for their children.

Each of these community schools was designed in response to children's academic needs as well as adults' needs as they affect student achievement. Each school acknowledges that schools are not just for children and that educating a child necessitates addressing every aspect of the child's life and environment. The concept of a community school greatly expands traditional notions of the purpose and function of schools in communities, and the role of teachers and school leaders within the school and community, as well as the community's responsibility for student success.

These cases provide feasible alternatives to traditional public schooling strategies that have not proven effective in rural communities and clearly underscore the challenge and opportunity for community schools to address the myriad issues facing rural communities.

Owsley Elementary and Middle School—Booneville, Kentucky

Owsley County Elementary School is located in Booneville, Kentucky, a stone's throw from where Daniel Boone and his party camped in 1780–81. It was called Boone's Station until Owsley County was organized in 1843, at which time it was renamed Booneville and became the county seat. Booneville's estimated population in 2008 was 105, down from 111 in the 2000 census.

Owsley County's population of 4,600 in 2008 is also down 4.6 percent since the 2000 census, and those residents are scattered over 198 square miles of the Eastern Coal Field Region. Almost the entire population (99.2 percent) is white. Fewer than half of adults 25 years old and older have a high school diploma. Median household income in 2007 was $21,189—52.6 percent of the national median of $40,299. Owsley ranks by many measures as the second poorest county in the United States with 44.4 percent of its residents in poverty. There are no industries, restaurants, or major highways in Owsley, and the school district is the largest employer.

Owsley County schools serve approximately 900 students in two facilities—Owsley County Elementary School (PK–6) and Owsley County High School (grades 7–12). One Christian school in the county enrolls 8 to 10 students. Owsley Elementary School enrolls about 400 students in Head Start, Early Head Start, and grades PK–6. The district operates two facilities, but it is by all counts a unified PK–12 school system. It is not unreasonable to think of Owsley as a community school system rather than a system with two community schools.

Superintendent Melinda Turner nearly chuckles when asked about school and community connections in Owsley County, saying, "The school is the community." Teachers, administrators, and community members echo this sentiment throughout the district. Nearly every important event in Owsley is held in the schools, including weddings, receptions, theatre performances, and emergency management.

Stephen Gebbard taught in the district twenty years before becoming principal of Owsley Elementary School. He is a graduate of Owsley County

High School, as are many of the district's teachers. The staff is acutely aware of the deep poverty affecting almost all of their students, but poverty is clearly not viewed as a reason for low expectations of either the students or the educators. In fact, poverty seems to be a motivator of staff commitment and resolve to see students succeed.

When asked how the district attained an obvious unity of vision for the success of its children, Gebbard said, "Folks realized that in order to facilitate education and address the physical, emotional, and social needs of students, you had to work with the entire community. In order to better the children, you have to better society." This realization can be attributed in large part to the strong, visionary leadership of the school principal, superintendent, and key staff.

When one enters Owsley Elementary School, there is nothing that reflects the deep and persistent poverty that plagues the community. The exterior wall of the Depression-era WPA-built gymnasium forms the interior, left wall of the warm, inviting entranceway. A safari theme runs throughout the building, creating a welcoming atmosphere for children and adults alike.

School and district leaders have leveraged scarce resources to provide a number of innovative programs, including a Save the Children Literacy Project, an Artist-in-Residence, Gifted and Talented Services, Reading First, and Everyday Mathematics. Superintendent Turner notes, "We apply for grants that others might think are not worth it," she said, "the $500 to $1,000 grants."

Owsley Elementary School has used a Leonore Annenberg School Fund grant provided through the Rural School and Community Trust to initiate a schoolwide technology program that puts iPods, iPads, and iMacs at the disposal of all students. The school principal, teachers, a parent, and district leaders in a team meeting during the researcher's site visit to Owsley talked excitedly about how they would use the technology to support student learning at all levels. Teachers, they said, would record mini-lessons and lectures for students who needed extra time and reinforcement. Books would be downloaded to give students access to texts that the school's budget could not afford. The technology would give students an eye to the world beyond Owsley and strengthen the already strong connections between the school and the community.

The school also offers a wide range of services to students and families in the community. Services are provided largely through the school's family resource center and the Quality Care for Kids program. A Youth Services Center provides similar services at the high school. It seems no one at Owsley Elementary School complains or thinks twice about going beyond their teaching duties to help children and families succeed.

Family Resource Center

Parents donated over 2,100 hours of volunteer service to Owsley Elementary School during the 2008–2009 school year, mostly through the family resource center. Teachers log their volunteer needs in the center, and the full-time center coordinator matches volunteers with the listed needs. Volunteering in the school has led a number of parents who dropped out of school to go back and complete their GEDs and higher-education degrees. Families can come into the center and get clothing, food, counseling, transportation to medical appointments, and even assistance in setting up utility payment plans when needed.

Health Services

The family resource center is also the door through which children and families access health services. The district pays about $5,000 per year per school for a school nurse and does Medicaid billing for students who qualify. The Quality Care for Kids program brings mobile clinics to the school for dental screenings and minor services and for hearing and vision screenings. The local Lions Club assists in purchasing eyeglasses when needed. The district participates in the Alliance for a Healthier Generation addressing health and wellness issues among students. The program was expanded recently to include staff and community health workers.

Kentucky Proud

Owsley's elementary students grow a pizza garden that provides vegetables for the school cafeteria. A Farm to School grant supports a high school gardening project, as well. Produce from the gardens is Kentucky Proud certified and sold in the local farmers' market.

Parent and Community Outreach

Owsley leverages its Title I program to strengthen its outreach to parents and the community. Ten monthly workshops a year provide information on health, academics, scholarship opportunities, and a host of other topics. The district's back-to-school event has become a "huge community event," drawing attendance from neighboring districts. The event includes a health fair and health screenings. The Labor Day week Community Fair features student exhibits and is attended by more than one thousand people, over a fourth of the community's four thousand residents. Steve Gebbard, the school principal, added, "The school system is the communication center for the community."

Molly Stark Elementary School—Bennington, Vermont

Bennington is a small rural village in southwestern Vermont surrounded by
the Green and Taconic Mountain ranges. It is a short commute from New
York City and the Berkshires of Massachusetts. The town's multiple historic
districts, mountain ranges, and covered bridges draw thousands of tourists
each year.

The town of Bennington is located in Bennington County. The county's
estimated population of 36,434 is 97.2 percent white. The median household
and per capita incomes are on par with the state as a whole, and poverty rates
in the county are slightly lower than in the state as a whole. Molly Stark
School is one of seven elementary schools in the Southwest Vermont Super-
visory Union. It is named after "Molly" Elizabeth Stark, remembered for her
support of her husband, General John Stark, and his troops during the
American Revolution. Her home functioned as a hospital, and she functioned
as a nurse to her husband's troops during a smallpox epidemic. It is little
wonder that the full-service community school that bears her name has a
major emphasis on providing health services to children and families who
need them.

Like all successful community schools, a key first step for Molly Stark
was planning. The school's principal and staff began in 1995 to consider
what they might do differently in response to the negative changes they had
seen in student behavior, parent involvement, and teacher morale. They began a series of focus group discussions among the school's staff, a physician,
a psychologist, and a police detective with whom they had worked over time
to determine what they might do to help children and families succeed.
Perhaps most important among the discussion topics was the question of the
school's beliefs about its role and responsibility in the lives of families and
with respect to student success.

Molly Stark's planning process spanned an entire school year of discussion and data collection. The data were used to determine what programs and
services children and families needed, how to provide them, and how to
obtain funding to implement and support them. Various data sources, including parent and community surveys, school and community data, and state
data were used to identify the most urgent needs.

Most outstanding among the school's findings was the fact that the district had the highest dropout rate in the state and the second highest teen
pregnancy rate. Medicaid-eligible students did not have adequate access to
dental services, and students were entering kindergarten unprepared to benefit from the experience. Those needs were then mapped to available resources and new program innovations that would make crucial child and
family services accessible and affordable. Having collected and assessed the

data, the Molly Stark team affiliated with the Yale Schools of the 21st Century program and began to move forward with its plan.

The result of the Molly Stark planning process is a full-service community school strategically focused on ensuring all students' success. The school began to implement its plan in 1996, staggering the initiation of services over several years. Services and programs have evolved in the years since, but are still strategically focused on meeting the multiple needs of its students and the families that care for them.

Family Center

Molly Stark's family center is the portal through which families access key services. The center employs a full-time home-school liaison who provides a "walking bus" through low-income housing areas near the school in the mornings and afternoons. She also focuses on attendance issues and follows up on tardies and early dismissals. Many of the health services provided by or facilitated through the school come under the family center's umbrella as well.

Health Services

Basic health services were among the initial services the school had planned to implement. They would bring on a dental hygienist who would make referrals to local dentists who agreed to treat Medicaid-eligible students. A retired dentist approached the school in 1998—one year into the program—with a proposal to begin an on-site dental practice for Medicaid-eligible students. Health services also include a pediatrician, an audiologist, and a psychologist who make regular visits to the school one or more days each week. A school nurse provides physical exams and inoculations for students with no primary care physician. The nurse also maintains a health office web page for parents and students. The site features monthly updates on important health topics, provides health and wellness information, and houses a variety of downloadable health care forms.

Molly Stark had to overcome many obstacles to establish the center. They had to first gain approval of the local school board to establish such a center. This is nearly an insurmountable hurdle in many rural areas where school boards and school leaders have become more focused on narrowing the school curriculum and preparing children to "pass the test." Molly Stark also was not an eligible applicant for the state grant that provides financial and technical assistance for needs assessment and planning in the areas of housing, economic development, public facilities, and services for low-income residents. The town's Select Board had to apply for the grant on the school's behalf. This situation could present clear and conflicting priorities in many rural towns, particularly where the leadership has a narrow vision of schools and does not see a clear connection between schools and broader economic development issues.

Molly Stark was able to overcome the hurdles and bring its family center and health services online. Medicaid covers many of the health services, but there remains a funding gap that the school has to fill with local resources to cover the time health professionals spend in the schools. This is a major challenge in the current budget crunch and with spiraling health care costs.

Day Care, Pre-school, and Kindergarten

Molly Stark operates an on-site licensed day care center that provides before and after school care beginning at 7:00 a.m. and ending at 5:30 p.m. Being a licensed center means that eligible families can receive child care subsidies and parents can pay for services on a sliding scale. Kindergarten care is available to morning and afternoon students, and integrated preschool services are provided four days a week. Staff members devote the fifth day to home visits. There are also summer and school vacation programs.

Family Development

Molly Stark offers a range of other family-strengthening services and programs in addition to health and child care. Parents can enroll in GED classes at the school one evening a week. Child care is available during these sessions, as are playgrounds for parents with infants and small children. The center also provides transportation and scholarships for GED testing. A Community Leadership Training program offered in conjunction with the Bennington County Child Care Association provides community members with education and experience in citizenship and advocacy for themselves and their children. Unlimited Fathering Opportunities provides dinner and recreational opportunities for fathers and their children ages three to six.

Other family strengthening programs include on-site community college courses taught by Molly Stark staff; adult and family literacy programs; a Family Lending Library with children's books, games, and videos; and a Cooking for Life program developed by the Vermont Campaign to End Childhood Hunger and the University of Vermont's Expanded Food and Nutrition Education program. This six-week program encourages parents and caregivers to prepare healthy, affordable meals.

Noble High School—North Berwick, Maine

Noble High School's guiding principle is that, "All students are capable of success; and all students will have the knowledge, skills and attitudes to become self-directed, lifelong learners; flexible workers; complex thinkers and responsible community and global contributors."

Noble High School is part of Maine's School Administrative District #60, or MSAD 60, which is a rural district in the southwestern county of York. York County was established in 1636 and has a rich fur trading and sawmills history. It is the oldest county in Maine, and one of the oldest in the United States. An estimated 201,876 people lived in York County in 2009, up 8.1 percent from the 2000 U.S. Census report. Almost all (97 percent) of the county's residents are white, with Hispanics making up the largest percentage (1.2 percent) of people of color. The county's median household income in 2008 was $54,626, which was higher than both the state ($46,419) and the national ($52,175) medians. Per capita income was also higher in the county than in the state as a whole, and the percentage of persons living below the poverty level was lower than in the state and nation (US Census Bureau, 2010).

York County's economic profile is skewed by the affluence of its most famous town, Kennebunkport. Kennebunkport has become a summer haven for the wealthy, including former President George H. W. Bush. But the three towns served by Noble High School—Berwick, North Berwick, and Lebanon—have different economic profiles. Two of the towns have median household incomes that are below the state median. According to the IES Center for Education Statistics, fewer than 10 percent of residents in the county live below the poverty level, but 21 percent of the school's students were eligible for free and reduced meals in 2008–2009.

Former principal Pam Fisher, speaking of the area surrounding Noble High School, commented, "A day's drive around our district would certainly convince anyone of the ubiquitous poverty." The towns have combined populations totaling 12,300 people, and the towns are rural but among the fastest growing areas in the state. There is no public transportation in any of the towns served by Noble High.

MSAD 60 serves approximately 3,000 students, about 1,070 of them at Noble High School in grades 9–12. The school and the community were facing a dilemma in 1995. The school had been built nearly 35 years earlier to accommodate 550 students, but its enrollment had grown to 900 and was growing by 50 to 100 students a year. The campus held 14 mobile units and could not accommodate the kinds of programs the school and community wanted for their children. The three towns that the school served were spread over 134 miles and lacking in basic services for both children and adults.

The need for a new school, combined with limited resources and mutual needs across the three towns, brought townspeople and educators together in an intensive eighteen-month planning process. Community members from all three towns participated in open forums, met with the principal at dinners and in private homes, and responded to surveys. A planning committee composed of school and community members identified three major goals to be accomplished with the construction of a new school: 1) build a sense of community among the three rural towns served by the school; 2) provide needed community services and lifelong learning opportunities for adults; and 3) create a more personal, project-based interdisciplinary learning environment for students.

The school's design was influenced by the towns' identified needs, the principles of the Coalition of Essential Schools, of which the school is a member, and the school district's guiding principles. The five design principles were:

- Abolish anonymity by creating small learning environments.
- Make spaces to reflect the concept of the teacher as coach, and the student as worker.
- Make sure the building supports a curriculum that is collaboratively designed, interdisciplinary, and project based.
- Create a school that serves as a community center and embraces community so that community functions are integrated with educational functions.
- Create a school that is flexible in design, materials, and function.

The result was a new Noble High School where the needs of both school and community are being met, and the lines between them are nearly indistinct. The school's main lobby is a "town square" where students, educators, and community members mingle. Then–Assistant Principal Tom Ledue noted in an interview with Rural Trust staffer Julie Bartsch that, "The design of our facility welcomes community members as well as our students. Parents that may not have particularly enjoyed their own high school experience have to notice a different feel to this school as soon as they walk through the front doors, one that is far more inviting than the one they remember."

Part of that welcome feel comes from the pictures and displays on the town square that are dedicated to and maintained by the three towns. The cases display local information, news, and histories of the towns. Streets lead from the town square to "educational neighborhoods" containing various learning communities, Head Start, a health center, a fifty-seat student-run restaurant, a one-thousand-seat performing arts center, and a cafeteria, all of which are used by both school and community groups.

Noble High School offers a rich and broad curriculum. Students must earn 24.5 credit hours to graduate, including five English, five math, four science, and one fine arts credits. The school has three academies, each consisting of heterogeneous groups of students in grades 9 through 12. All students must complete a common curriculum. Students must build portfolios connecting their work to Maine's Learning Results and do a project-based presentation. Other learning opportunities are provided through participation on the Civil Rights Team, on the school board, and in a wide variety of school clubs.

Comprehensive Health Services

A partnership with the York County Hospital provides Noble with a nurse practitioner during school hours. The school-based health center sees about 100 to 150 students a month. The nurse practitioner and school nurses triage services with the hospital and local physicians. Services were initially provided at no cost to students and their families, but increased staff, maintenance, and utilities costs have led to charges for some services. Student services include diagnosis and treatment of acute illness and injury; management of chronic ailments, including asthma and diabetes; routine hearing, visual, and dental screenings; prescription services; laboratory testing; sports examinations; and mental health services.

Early Childhood Programs

Noble houses two early childhood programs: Head Start and Early Childhood. Children come from eight surrounding towns and attend at no cost. The programs provide internships and work-study opportunities for high school students enrolled in the school's early childhood education program.

Performing Arts Center

Noble's one-thousand-seat performing arts center was funded in part through a referendum passed by the three towns. The center houses a theater, an auditorium, and a small lecture hall. A group of community members serves as the center's advisory board. The center is available for many functions at no cost to the community, but rental and admissions fees have made it financially self-sustaining.

Culinary Arts

Noble houses the Stanford Vocational Culinary Arts Program, which shares space with the school kitchen. Students in the two-year program operate a fifty-person restaurant that is open during school hours and accessible from the town square. The restaurant, like the town square, is a gathering place for students, teachers, and community members.

Community Service

Noble's students must complete sixty hours of community service. Service opportunities are posted on the school's website. The community service program reflects the school's commitment "to its students to heighten their sense of global responsibility, their sensitivity to social problems, . . . and a sense of personal fulfillment through their commitment and caring for others."

Adult Education

The Adult Continuing Education Center offers on-site and online classes and teleconferences for students and community members. Noble's students provide full-day child care for parents enrolled in the program.

CONCLUSION

Rural schools enroll more than 10 million of our nation's children. The rural places where these children live are economically, culturally, and religiously diverse, as are the students themselves. This diversity in place and people makes it unlikely that a single community school model will work in all rural settings. This is, perhaps, the most important lesson to be drawn from the three cases presented here.

The word "community" in full-service community schools implies more than those services or activities that normally happen outside of the school setting. It implies a uniqueness about place and the people who live there. Each place has a unique history, culture, economy, and ecology. Each has a unique set of relationships, power structures, challenges, and opportunities. We must therefore plan each community school taking into account its individual surroundings and circumstances.

Successful community schools do not come about merely by co-locating services. Planning a successful community school is an intensive process that involves multiple stakeholders, as was the case with the construction of a new Noble High School. Planning is just as essential and intensive when new construction is not in the picture, as was the case with Molly Stark and Owsley elementary schools.

Transformational change in the delivery of public education requires not just a narrow focus on education, but also a keen focus, intentionality, and broad-based collaboration around addressing the needs of children and families. It requires broad-based consensus building and merging of institutional and organizational cultures. An intermediary that is not vested in local politics is in many cases best suited to facilitate this kind of planning. Funding for strategic community school planning is a worthwhile investment of public dollars.

The result of planning that takes into account the uniqueness of place and people is that each community school offers curricular, co-curricular, and family and community services that are specific to the needs of the community it serves. They reflect both what the state requires and what local people want for their children and community—a one-thousand-seat performing arts center and a foreign student exchange program at Noble; comprehensive health services and a community leadership training program at Molly Stark; and Kentucky Proud vegetable gardens and assistance with family members' transportation to medical appointments at Owsley, for example.

Community schools are in many ways a natural phenomenon in highly stressed rural communities such as Owsley County. The school is the greatest resource in the community, the largest employer, and custodian of the largest public facilities. Leadership plays a crucial role in developing a common vision and high expectations for what is possible, notwithstanding circumstance. The kind of leadership that principals and superintendents in the case studies exhibit seems more often to be the exception than the rule. There are strong implications here for university-based school leadership programs. These programs should embrace the community school concept and immediately begin to integrate preparation for leadership in community schools into their curricula and internships for aspiring rural school leaders.

State education agencies also should embrace and promote the community school concept in rural communities, both as an alternative to consolidation and as a school turnaround strategy. Assistance teams assigned to struggling schools should be well versed in the community school concept and able to facilitate a community school planning process in targeted schools.

This study focuses primarily on the benefits of community schools in highly stressed rural communities. Yet many of the highlighted characteristics of community schools can be applied in traditional school settings with little to no cost. School boards can remove policies that inhibit parent and community engagement. Schools can partner with community colleges to provide educational services that bring adults into the school building such as adult literacy, English as a second language, college courses, and career and technical certification programs. School districts can partner with recreation departments, arts councils, historic societies, and other community resources to make facilities available to students and community members beyond normal school hours. State departments can convene discussions with other state agencies to remove barriers to joint-use facilities and make the regulations around facility construction and use more uniform.

State and federal policies and grant programs can be powerful enablers for the spread of rural community schools. Our current economic crisis and the concurrent crisis in public education provide the challenge, opportunity, and necessity to consider the community school concept more seriously and implement it more broadly.

NOTE

1. Adapted from 2010 white paper, published by Center for American Progress.

Chapter Seven

Leading STEM in the Community School Setting

Judith Dymond

School districts throughout the nation are faced with major changes as we all work toward educational reform and set goals to increase achievement through student engagement. One direction that many districts are taking is enhanced and integrated STEM instruction. Indeed, the Common Core Standards (CCS) have aided this shift, but many states have also additionally adopted the *Next Generation Science Standards* (NGSS). Undoubtedly, STEM is a national trend, and many districts are considering reorganizing course offerings and exploring new ways to excite children about these fields at earlier ages.

Though some educators will attempt to pursue these goals independently, wise school leaders are looking to the greater community to help accomplish these goals. Each community has its own unique set of resources available; the traditional resources, such as state and federal funding mechanisms, do not seem sufficient for most districts. In this chapter, leaders will learn first steps for developing relationships and partnerships, ways to manage these connections, and ways to sustain these collaborations—all for the purpose of STEM education.

WHY IS STEM EDUCATION IMPORTANT?

It takes the whole community to assist students as they set their career goals. In a summer school program for middle school students, one middle school student shared that his career goal was to be a football player in the NFL. When asked about other career options he had thought about, he had none.

Clearly it takes more than a family to illuminate career options and life goals for children. Indeed, being a football player in the NFL is a great aspiration, and perhaps he will make it there one day. Yet in our ever-changing economy, everyone needs a backup plan. While career choices may seem premature at middle school age, I would argue that career aspirations give students a sense of what is possible. Exposing students to STEM fields is a new challenge for schools. In the past, many students left the K–12 setting without knowing anything about engineering. If a student isn't exposed to these fields at an early age, he or she cannot consider these careers.

According to the Department of Education's statistics, "only 16% of American high school seniors are proficient in mathematics and interested in a STEM career . . . only half of the students who pursue STEM studies actually pursue careers in STEM fields. The United States ranks 29th in mathematics and 22nd in science among industrialized nations." STEM education has thus been encouraged as a means for the United States to increase its global competitiveness.

According to the U.S. Congress Joint Economic Committee (JEC), between 2010 and 2020, the overall employment in STEM occupations will increase by 17 percent. Yet, currently, there are two science and technology job openings for every qualified job seeker. Added to this, there is a lack of gender and ethnic diversity of students entering STEM fields. Only 2 percent of the workforce in STEM fields is Hispanic. Hispanic and white students are equally likely to major in STEM fields, but Hispanics are significantly less likely to earn a degree or certificate. Furthermore, according to White House statistics, 16 percent of the Hispanic students who began college in 2004 in a STEM field graduated with a STEM degree in 2009.

To address the shortage of U.S. STEM-trained students, the U.S. Department of Education has developed the Five-Year Federal Science, Technology, Engineering, and Math (STEM) Strategic Plan to improve Pre-K–12 instruction, increase and sustain youth and public engagement with STEM, enhance undergraduate STEM education, create STEM graduate fellowships, and better serve groups historically underrepresented in STEM fields. The development of the plan came as a result of President Obama's statement in 2010 that "Leadership tomorrow depends on how we educate our students today—especially in science, technology, engineering, and math." The plan was to expose students to STEM education and STEM careers at an earlier age, as early as preschool.

Universities and colleges are mobilizing around those initiatives that present a challenge to K–12 school districts. Opportunities abound by partnering with these educational institutions. By connecting to educational institutions, nonprofits, and corporations, school districts expand their networks. Every partner has its own network.

THE ROLE OF THE COMMUNITY IN STEM EDUCATION

Many states are using the *Next Generation Science Standards* (NGSS) as the model for their state-adopted science standards. The NGSS framework is an evidence-based model that aids in conceptual theory building regarding scientific knowledge at developmentally appropriate stages. There are three dimensions to NGSS: (a) practices that describe behaviors that scientists engage in as they investigate and build models and the key set of engineering practices that engineers use as they design and build models and systems; (b) crosscutting concepts which have application across all domains of science; and (c) disciplinary core ideas which focus on the most important aspects of science. The three dimensions (science and engineering practices, core science content, and crosscutting concepts which extend over all STEM core content) are intended to make STEM education more relevant to students' daily experiences by engaging them in interactive lessons and real-life career connections.

What better way to demonstrate to students how the STEM fields relate to everyday life than by connecting directly to the community? Why should districts try to create experiences when exemplary STEM programs may already exist within the community? While districts are focused on core science content and making connections across disciplines with crosscutting concepts, they should also take advantage of the resources in local corporations, small businesses, universities, and other institutions. Doing so will dramatically increase students' exposure to real careers.

To prepare children to be career and college ready, families must be supported. In the process of identifying external stakeholders/community partners, it is important to identify partners that are already addressing the needs of families—for instance, local community colleges offering GED classes, YMCAs that offer after-school opportunities, churches and other religious organizations that are already hosting activities for teens, and so forth.

Engaging the greater community in the educational process should be systematic. School leaders must identify the resources that will support STEM education, develop a systems approach to communication, build trust internally and externally to sustain the relationships, and engage the community strategically. This process begins with district leaders assessing community resources and identifying those entities that can connect STEM meaningfully to students. To do this, building principals and central office staff need to be good listeners as they gather data from interviews and observation, or bring together groups of community representatives to brainstorm how they might provide support. Ideally, it should be a leadership goal for the district, as STEM education needs to start early. As such, a plan can be devised for approaching the potential resource organizations and individuals in the greater community.

First and foremost, the community needs to be educated so that it can understand the types of support that the district seeks. Depending on the size of the district, it could be the superintendent, a central office leader, or the building principal. One suggestion would be to have an administrator address local organizations such as the Chamber of Commerce or the Rotary Club. Another approach would be to pull together a group of nonprofit organizations in town to share the need for STEM connections, to find out where they are impacting families, and to share networks on a regular basis. The possibilities are endless, but the point remains that these opportunities must be presented to companies and service organizations in an organized and understandable fashion. The ultimate message that must be communicated is that this partnership is to help children be successful.

Once the word has been shared in a variety of locations, administrators need to determine who already has made a connection to these organizations and individuals. Often, it is someone on the leadership team, as many live in the community. Before initiating these connections and developing relationships, it is good to discuss potential barriers in the process. Engaging the community in a manner that builds trust and is sustainable takes pre-planning to avoid pitfalls. These barriers or roadblocks can change in different stages of the community engagement process: developing, implementing, and sustaining of initiatives and partnerships.

Cox-Peterson, Melber, and Patchen (2012) suggest that management is a key roadblock; time must be set aside to recruit members of the community, to coordinate, to plan, and to assign specific tasks. Mentioning this goal at weekly administrative team meetings and assigning team members to coordinate such efforts is critical. Glanz (2006) suggests several further possible roadblocks for engaging the community such as fear of public scrutiny, staff burnout, and negative attitudes about the community. Yet successful leaders must take risks. By engaging the community, leaders have opportunities for face-to-face conversations about goals and strategies for meeting district obligations. Furthermore, community members learn where they can apply their resources and support the district in a variety of ways. By being part of the process, they also learn some of the obstacles that the district is facing, and teachers and administrators realize the positives. Having one designated person to consistently be the contact has worked for the university with its community and school contacts. It saves time for both parties. It also prevents miscommunication.

IDENTIFYING COMMUNITY RESOURCES

Every community has a remarkably different set of resources. Particularly in the case of a STEM initiative, effective educational leaders expand their circles to find meaningful connections for young people to learn about STEM careers and excite them about these fields of study. A network can be expanded by collaborating with other institutions, such as technical schools, junior colleges, and universities. Every nonprofit organization, business, and educational institution has its own network and will be able to help districts connect students to STEM in the real world.

Whenever one institution chooses to partner with another organization, both organizations should gain from the partnership and both should be held accountable. Before initiating the contact, it is good to learn about the organization and its mission. Companies often want to have their employees directly involved and certainly want positive publicity. Mayors, chambers of commerce, Rotary clubs, and Kiwanis clubs are good places to start. Additionally, parents make good resources. They may be connected to STEM-related corporations or local businesses. It is particularly meaningful to hear from professionals in the community; students more likely will realize that such careers are attainable goals for them.

STEM corporations might make school visits or allow tours of their facilities. Small businesses often have projects that they cannot find time to complete or do not have the expertise to solve a particular problem. School teams could be put on these projects, which would give them real experience and help the small business remain in the community. Universities use these strategies to prepare students for transitions to their careers. Depending on the project, middle and high school students might be able to work in teams to solve these small business problems. Finally, nearby colleges and universities have the capacity to pull together educational institutions, nonprofits, businesses, and corporations and to facilitate discussions about ways to connect students to STEM in the real world.

THE ROLE OF THE UNIVERSITY FOR
COMMUNITY ORGANIZING

Universities serve as a solid resource for school districts in providing programming opportunities for teachers, students, and parents; however, more importantly, the university has the capacity for pulling the community together around a cause. For instance, universities intentionally hire staff for the purpose of community engagement. They connect to businesses for strategic reasons. They are in the center of much community life, as their institutional legitimacy comes from the continued attraction of institutions to the university.

If there is a university near the school district, both the university and the school district can benefit from a partnership. Universities have the capacity to organize key leaders in the greater community around STEM education and STEM careers. In many cases, a university will connect with the community to aid economic growth. Universities in particular partner with businesses and local governments in order to stimulate growth, provide internships, serve as a resource for start-up companies, and arrange for students to problem-solve for the various challenges faced by small businesses.

One example is the state of Illinois, which is leading a STEM initiative designed to support college and career readiness for learners and to better prepare them for transitions into employment. Universities are hosting these meetings by bringing together education partners and employers throughout the state. *STEM Learning Exchanges* have been formed around selected career clusters to improve the coordination and delivery of resources, work-based learning opportunities, career guidance, and partnerships that support local STEM programs. Lead designated organizations, such as universities, workforce development initiatives, and educational foundations are responsible for coordinating a network of businesses, employer associations, and educators throughout the state.

Universities are also contributing to the Learning Registry which is compiling STEM Open Educational Resources (OER). OERs are freely accessible, openly licensed materials for teaching, learning, and assessment purposes. The materials can be used without cost and modified without violating any copyright laws. There are several national initiatives from which to choose. Universities also offer STEM summer camps and other outreach programming to stimulate interest in STEM careers. Northern Illinois University, for example, offers residential summer camps for middle school and high school students to explore STEM fields in a variety of areas: engineering, chemistry, coding, green technology, biology, health care, nanotechnology, and video game design, to name a few.

Finally, universities are connected to foundations and often have alumni who are willing and able to fund camps for underserved young people. They have programs to support underserved students as they pursue an academic career. Pursuing STEM education is important, but more important is completing the course of study.

STARTING EARLY: NEVER TOO EARLY

Exposure to STEM fields can begin as early as preschool. A good strategy is to engage parents in ways that allow them to learn about such fields along with their children. Afterschool events for preschool and elementary children which provide hands-on science exploration involving both the parent and child can help lay the foundation for STEM education. Another strategy is to invite diverse community members in STEM fields into classrooms. Students can more easily imagine themselves in these fields if they seem attainable; seeing people within their own communities who have attained these goals makes it seem more plausible.

University outreach and STEM departments may be able to provide STEM demonstrations at schools or provide hands-on activities from the variety of science fields. Universities and colleges offer STEM summer camps and may have scholarships based on need. Counselors are able to connect underserved students to these foundations and donors to provide funding for promising students to attend camps on STEM careers.

The Council for Economic Education, in particular, provides resources and teacher training to expose young children to financial literacy and the economic way of thinking. They deliver this training and offer competitive programs for students and teachers which exposes students to financial careers and develops decision-making skills to transition students to the real world and to college and careers. The council delivers these math-related opportunities through its state affiliates and in turn through the state centers which are usually housed in universities. Some university centers have provided resources and professional development to Y providers to enhance their after-school programs.

Universities are connected to local libraries and often offer STEM programming in conjunction with each other. Libraries, particularly those that draw from diverse populations, can secure funding for a variety of educational programs. Every educator should make a friend of the local librarian. Children's literature today is abundant with fiction books connected to STEM topics and a multitude of fine informational texts on STEM topics for children at a variety of reading levels. Educators are allowed to check out large quantities of books for their classrooms from most libraries. Learning about STEM through the arts is a very popular concept today.

HOW COMMUNITY RESOURCES CAN INFLUENCE GENDER EQUITY IN STEM

Females are another underrepresented group in the science fields that school districts will want to engage. According to the National Girls Collaborative statistics which are taken from the U.S. Department of Labor, Bureau of Labor Statistics, *Women in the Labor Force: A Databook, 2014*, women make up 47 percent of the total workforce. However, in particular, in science and engineering occupations, they report that women are much less represented. The statistics are as follows:

- 39 percent of chemists and material scientists are women;
- 27.9 percent of environmental scientists and geoscientists are women;
- 15.6 percent of chemical engineers are scientists;
- 12.1 percent of civil engineers are women;
- 8.3 percent of electrical and electronics engineers are women; and
- 17.2 percent of industrial engineers are women.

Further statistics indicate that race and ethnicity are also indicators of participation in science and engineering. National Science Foundation indicators show that minority women comprise fewer than one in ten employed scientists and engineers.

School leaders should connect parents, after-school organizations, children's group leaders, and educators to the National Girls Collaborative Project (NGCP) for resources. These advocates can network and share ideas and strategies for exciting girls about STEM fields. Additionally, universities and communities working together can find mentors in STEM fields for girls. The Northern Illinois University STEM Outreach program has an initiative for girls called STEM Divas. STEM Divas engages girls by embracing their femininity and involving the girls in STEM activities to emphasize that girls can pursue the science careers and be feminine. They wear pink helmets and vests and use pink tools to produce some very interesting projects.

Another resource for educators, group leaders, and parents which promotes STEM fields to girls is *SciGirls*. *SciGirls* is a PBS show for kids ages 8–12. The show's website features games, activities, tips for science clubs, and plenty of videos with girls engaged in fun science activities. The goal of *SciGirls* is to change how millions of girls think about science, technology, engineering, and math.

SUSTAINING COMMUNITY ENGAGEMENT

We have explored in detail many of the programs and organizations that districts can connect with to promote STEM to K–12 students. After determining which programs best meet the needs of the community and the school district, the district leader needs to create an environment of sustainable community engagement featuring systematic communication.

Timely communication is critical to building trust among organizations and community partners. It is important for leaders to be systematic in communicating with partners, especially with large institutions such as universities, city governments, and corporations. Building trust means that there are no surprises. Because these institutions are large, it is a good strategy to channel information through a limited number of sources who need to be in communication with each other. Communication must be systematic and timely within the district and with its external partners.

Systematic communication is the key to ensuring a consistent message comes from the school district. Depending on the size of the district, the superintendent may not be the one who is making the connections, but the superintendent needs to be kept informed and make sure these goals are repeated at administrative meetings. Too often administrators move on or their responsibilities change; others need to be informed about what has transpired.

To successfully engage the community, "the 'engage' needs to be reciprocal . . . if the district wants to engage key members of the community, the school leader also must be willing to serve on other committees and be involved actively in community events . . . to serve on the United Way Board . . . serve on the Education Foundation . . . which includes community and business leaders, so you stay engaged" (Dymond 2014, p. 58). So the strategy of the leader is to serve on existing community committees rather than developing new committees or advisory boards. Leaders find it beneficial to connect building principals to community projects that interest them.

Effective management of community engagement goes hand in hand with the development of relationships. "The most significant impact . . . on developing a partnership is the relationship between the individual . . . and the principal/educator responsible for the task" (Dymond, 2014). Progress reports at administrative and community partnership meetings by both school leaders and community members hold people accountable. Some superintendents and school leaders require administrative team leaders to report on implementation of the engagement plan as part of their evaluation.

Shared leadership is key to the success of programs and initiatives. When community members are engaged in shared decision-making, programs and initiatives are sustained. After interviewing superintendents, it is clear that excellent superintendents are involving their communities on a variety of levels and can document engagement of the community in the decision-making process. They unanimously believed that it was beneficial to devote time to engaging the community. Those superintendents who kept goals in front of the community and staff were most successful in implementing goals. School districts cannot go it alone. There are too many concerns for educators in this time of economic challenge and school reform. Expecting results and accountability assures that partnerships will be sustained.

Hank Rubin (2002) who wrote extensively about collaborative leadership, recommended, "Cultivating partners shouldn't end once they commit to the partnership. Cultivation of partners . . . requires ongoing attention . . . effective collaboration happens between people—one person at a time" (p. 106).

Through my interactions with superintendents, I discovered that there is not one set procedure or way to engage the community. The strategies depend on the specific community since every community is in a different place. When the superintendents of the school districts talked about community engagement, they included university partnerships, parent involvement, and engaging specific community entities under the same umbrella. Cox-Peterson, Melber, and Patchen (2012) suggest that community does not just refer to the physical place, but to the relationship among the people involved in the partnership.

Community members need to know that what they have done benefited students. There needs to be a time set aside to celebrate collaboration. Having children demonstrate what they have learned at these functions is motivating. This rang through recently at a fund-raiser for economic education. Within minutes of a video in which a young child was demonstrating what he knew about financial literacy, the fund-raising doubled. People need to come full circle and see the results of their efforts for sustainability. Be patient. It takes time to make lasting changes.

Chapter Eight

Preparing Aspiring Leaders for Community School Leadership

Karen Carlson

In this chapter, stepping back from the daily struggles of school leadership, I discuss the skill sets and professional knowledge needed for effective community school leadership. This can be used by leaders for their own professional development plans, or by educational administration faculty members to design curriculum for aspiring school leaders. What would it take to lead a community-based school? What knowledge, skills, and dispositions does one need? And how can these things be developed?

NEW PROFESSIONAL STANDARDS FOR SCHOOL LEADERS

Timing matters. On October 23, 2015, the National Policy Board for Educational Administration (NPBEA), the umbrella organization for the major professional organizations responsible for teacher and leadership education (Council of Chief State School Officers, CAEP, NAESP, NASSP, UCEA, NCPEA, AASA, NBPTS), unanimously approved new standards for all educational leaders. Formerly known as the ISLLC (the Interstate School Leaders Licensure Consortium) standards which have guided the training, development, and evaluation of school and district level leaders across the United States since 1996, the new standards take into account pivotal educational research conducted over the past twenty years. Instead of the original six leadership standards, there are now ten. Taken from a synthesis of the research on leadership and school improvement, there is an acknowledgment that certain foundational principles of leadership are necessary to educate *all* children to high standards in the twenty-first century. Interestingly, the new standards align to practices that successful community school principals have implemented all along, many of which have *not* been part of traditional leadership training. This suggests that training and development of future school leaders will shift significantly in the coming years. It is my belief that a model of schooling more closely aligned to the community school model will prevail, primarily because it aligns with the new standards.

THEORY OF ACTION: HOW LEADERSHIP PRACTICE INFLUENCES STUDENT ACHIEVEMENT

The National Policy Board groups the 2015 standards into four domains or clusters that are interdependent and build a theory of action for how educational leader practice influences student achievement (NPBEA, 2015, pp. 4–5). The standards do not work in isolation; in other words, for best results, schools need to work on academic goals in conjunction with socio-emotional supports to ensure success. The clusters are as follows:

Cluster One
Standard 4: Curriculum, Instruction and Assessment
Standard 5: Community of Care and Support for Students
Cluster Two
Standard 6: Professional Capacity of School Personnel
Standard 7: Professional Community for Teachers and Staff
Standard 8: Meaningful Engagement of Families and Community
Standard 9: Operations and Management
Cluster Three
Standard 1: Mission, Vision and Core Values
Standard 2: Ethics and Professional Norms
Standard 3: Equity and Cultural Responsiveness
Cluster Four
Standard 10: School Improvement

In cluster 1, Curriculum, Instruction and Assessment is supported by a strong Community of Care and Support for Students. This refers to a school culture where every child is known, accepted, and valued; where a safe, caring, healthy environment that fosters the child's emotional, physical, social, and academic needs is developed; where extracurricular activities are offered that nurture the whole child; accommodations and modifications are available to ensure academic and behavioral success, languages and cultures are infused, relationships are honored.

In cluster 2, leaders develop the capacity of teachers and staff to meet the needs of students; build a safe, trusting community for teachers and staff; engage families and community in meaningful, reciprocal, and mutually beneficial ways to promote *each* student's academic success and well-being.

They create structures and systems to support the organization, and all are intertwined. These are priorities and actions that community school leaders use to effect change.

In cluster 3, the shared mission, vision, and core values relate to holding strong professional ethics and norms of behavior. This is tied closely to a community school leader's struggle for social justice, ensuring that students are treated fairly and equitably, confronting low expectations associated with race, class, culture, language, gender and sexual orientation, and/or disability or special status. A culturally competent leadership style is expected. Once again, the community school leadership model resonates with these standards.

In summary, students learn best when leaders foster safe and caring learning communities and promote rigorous curricula, instruction, and assessment systems. Continuous improvement loops that gather data, involve constituents in the process, assess progress toward goals regularly, and redirect work based on data affect outcomes.

CHANGES TO THE STANDARDS AND THEIR IMPACT ON LEADERSHIP DEVELOPMENT

Leaders cannot only care about reading, writing, and arithmetic. They must care about the whole child, and with the whole child comes the whole family and his or her community. The ultimate goal is a healthy child in a healthy family, embedded in a healthy community. The four standards listed above were not in the 1996 or 2008 ISLLC standards that have defined leadership training and development for the past twenty years. The new standards respond to increasing evidence that emphasizes the importance of the social aspects of education. The new standards are as follows:

- Standard 3: Equity and Cultural Responsiveness
- Standard 5: Community of Care and Support for Students
- Standard 6: Professional Capacity of School Personnel
- Standard 7: Professional Community for Teachers and Staff

The new standards expect school leaders to promote an understanding and appreciation of the school's cultural, social, and intellectual diversity. Leaders are expected to build positive relationships with families and students' guardians and address issues of "student marginalization; deficit-based schooling." They are also expected to limit "assumptions about gender, race, class, and special status," and promote cultural understanding (Superville, 2015).

The new language around family and community engagement is exciting. Instead of top-down approaches to parent involvement, the 2015 language demands that "effective educational leaders engage families and the community in meaningful, reciprocal and mutually beneficial ways to promote each student's academic success and well being" (National Policy Board for Educational Administration, 2015, p. 16). The research bears out what community school proponents have been advocating for years: Principals must support the whole child and family to maximize learning. Issues of race, poverty, and context matter. When principals bring community partners in to work together to co-create and share the vision for the community, everyone grows, thrives, and succeeds. Additionally, principals need to build staff capacity to work effectively with parents and the community, all based on trust. Many principals are not trained to do this type of work. Those engaged in training aspiring, novice, and even experienced school leaders will have to build a new repertoire of skills and experiences to better engage with communities. The most effective experiences will have been interdisciplinary and community-based.

MINDSET AND DISPOSITIONS

In the Model Policy Standards for Educational Leaders Draft for Public Comment, May 11–29, 2015 (CCSSO 2015), eight dispositions of Transformational Educational Leaders were outlined that undergird the standards. These dispositions also inform the work of transformational community school principals and leaders. The dispositions are as follows:

- Growth-oriented: Transformational education leaders believe that students, education professionals, educational organizations, and the community can continuously grow and improve to realize a shared vision for student success through dedication and hard work.
- Collaborative: Transformational education leaders share the responsibility and the work for realizing a shared vision of student success.
- Innovative: Transformational education leaders break from established ways of doing things to pursue fundamentally new and more effective approaches when needed.
- Analytical: Transformational education leaders gather evidence and engage in rigorous data analysis to develop, manage, refine, and evaluate new and more effective approaches.
- Ethical: Transformational education leaders explicitly and consciously follow laws, policies, and principles of right and wrong in everything they do.

- Perseverant: Transformational education leaders are courageous and persevere in doing what is best for students even when challenged by fear, risk, and doubt.
- Reflective: Transformational education leaders reexamine their practices and dispositions habitually in order to develop the "wisdom of practice" needed to succeed in pursuing new and more effective approaches.
- Equity-minded: Transformational education leaders ensure that all students are treated fairly and equitably and have access to excellent teachers and necessary resources.

Belief systems are hard to change. A leader must believe that all stakeholders (students, professionals, educational organizations, and the community) can continuously grow and improve and that a shared, collaborative vision for student success is needed. Some school leaders do not regard community members as equals, but in a community school, one must. A principal of a community school believes that the school serves the entire learning community and all members should grow and thrive. By developing family and community members as well as the children, the entire enterprise improves. Further, the leader must develop the skills to foster, cultivate, and maintain a shared vision, including the faculty, families, and community residents. All adults are responsible and accountable for student success. The leader must access the community, listen to what the various stakeholders say, and include them in planning and executing the vision and mission of the school. Adult learning needs are also reflected in the community school design to help constituents thrive.

Community school leaders develop a distributed leadership model which includes community partners and parents who share responsibility for realizing the vision. They build an infrastructure across the community for shared leadership and responsibility for student success. Knowing how to build trust and two-way partnerships is a skill that successful school leaders need. The *2015 Standards for School Leaders* reflects the importance of cultivating leadership capacity in others, recognizing that leadership is not the sole province of the principal. Building a strong collaborative team is a key to successful community school leadership.

Community school leaders are naturally "out of the box thinkers" who do not follow traditional methods of working with families and communities, primarily because those methods have not been effective. The question is how to bring your community to think outside of the box also? It is said that those closest to the problem are best able to solve their problems; community school leaders work with cross-functional teams to create innovative solutions to their problems. Community school leaders see their buildings as more than a school that operates Monday–Friday from 8:00 a.m.–4:00 p.m. They see their school building as a community resource, an asset to be used during nonschool hours for other functions as tutoring, social services, health services, open gym, organized sports, meeting space, GED, ESL, job training, and counseling. Because classrooms are used outside of school hours, teachers have to be flexible and tolerant of others using their space; the before or after-school hours teacher has to honor the classroom teacher's belongings and materials. Community school principals are entrepreneurial risk takers, as are their team members.

Leaders examine qualitative and quantitative data to determine whether programs work. There are no sacred cows. In a community school, a principal is able to show data to different constituents in simple ways understood by all. They know how to organize and hold data summits, analyze data, break it down to show trends, use data to make difficult decisions, and help others to do the same. They are able to give a "state of the school" message that is easily understandable by multiple constituents and available in many languages. They are willing to analyze their own work, successes, and shortcomings in a transparent manner, confront data with a thick skin, and reflect and revise strategies if outcomes do not demonstrate success. They should be able to transform data into stories that everyday people can understand and relate to easily.

Community school leaders model ethical behavior in action, word, and thought. Leaders should ask themselves, "Am I comfortable with this decision printed on the front page of the newspaper?" They understand the political process and know how laws and policies can be changed when they are not equitable or do not serve the community; they know how to lobby decision-makers and work for social justice. The lack of trust that many community residents have developed with regard to their local schools and governmental agencies has to be repaired. By behaving in an ethical, transparent, and open manner consistently, community school leaders can rebuild trust.

Community school leaders make decisions based on what is *best for children*. For example, in Comer School Development Program schools use placards with the question, "Is this best for children?" at every team meeting. Principals must stay the course and not be pushed to change strategy because of political pressure. Bold school leaders courageously work for change and stick to their principles for the long haul. They must be willing to defend their practices and show data to demonstrate stories of success. They must remain mindful that politicians often pressure principals for quick fixes but schools do not improve overnight.

Community school leaders are reflective practitioners who reflect in action, continually seeking to improve their practice each day. They seek feedback and develop a thick skin to receive and grow from constructive comments. Bold leaders are not defensive when presented with information that is not complimentary or suggests that they need to rework something. They welcome feedback because it signals people feel comfortable to tell them the truth; that they are partners in the continuous improvement process. Leaders are willing to say they have made a mistake. To realize the school's vision of student learning and stay true to the school's core values, educational leaders subject every realm of the school to improvement, including themselves and their work. This builds credibility. They build a culture of reflective practice within the entire community by modeling.

Community school leaders lead the struggle for social justice to level the playing field. They confront difficult issues and hold conversations about race and class, ask for evidence and data, strive for equity, and work relentlessly to ensure that their students and community get the best teachers and resources. The culturally competent schools where all constituents are honored, respected, valued, and included. They confront issues such as mediocrity, racism, gender equity, bullying, and classism. Finally, educationally effective leaders believe their schools can always be better. "They are tenacious change agents who are creative, inspirational and willing to weather the potential risks, uncertainties and political fall-out to make their schools places where each student thrives." (NPBEA, 2015, p. 4.)

WHAT DO COMMUNITY SCHOOL LEADERS NEED TO SUCCESSFULLY LEAD SCHOOLS OF TOMORROW?

Several studies have been conducted asking successful community school leaders what they need to be successful—in particular, things that did not come from their regular principal preparation training. Broadly, some of the categories mentioned include working effectively with parents and the community, sharing power, political training, financing community schools, working with community-based organizations, conflict management, marketing, using data to tell stories, fund-raising and grantwriting, networking, building multilevel infrastructure, systems thinking, diversity training, and cultural competence, among others (Blank, Berg & Melaville, 2006).

The new leadership standards address all the critical development needs of community school leaders, be it during the principal preparation phase as part of a university training program, an alternative certification route, a school district's strategic focus or as part of an individual school leader's personal professional development plan. Many professors or professional developers who have not led community schools themselves may have difficulty teaching some of these concepts effectively. For this reason, a multidisciplinary approach to the preparation of school leaders would be beneficial rather than having professors or professional developers from a school of education exclusively. Courses or workshops should be taught or cotaught by researchers and practitioners in different fields including but not limited to education, psychology, social work, economics, law, medicine, politics, business, and community organizing, to gain multiple perspectives. Community school leaders are boundary crossers and this interdisciplinary approach will serve them well.

The Professional Standards for Educational Leaders 2015 are listed at the end of this chapter. What follows here is a discussion of their relevance to a community school principal's leadership repertoire and ideas for development.

Creating a Shared Vision

Engage stakeholders. Public engagement is an essential component of community schools. It comes from consistent efforts to engage not only parents, but all segments of the community and involve them in community decision-making. It gives citizens a voice in crafting solutions that reflect their own preferences and values. To continue to build community support for schools, community principals must continually demonstrate how their schools benefit and incorporate the preferences, resources, and best interests of all the local citizens (Blank, Berg & Melaville, 2006).

Listening campaign. In building a shared vision, a leader should initiate a listening campaign to learn what internal and external stakeholders think about their school, its community, its strengths, and its needs. The leader has to understand the core values of stakeholders while providing them with a clear understanding of his or her commitment to child-centered education, high expectations, equity, inclusiveness, and social justice. The listening campaign builds relationships and captures qualitative data that reveals connecting opportunities based on the community's assets (Kretzmann and McKnight, 1993). The goal of the listening campaign is to look for ways to connect, show what the school could bring to the relationships, and uncover ways the school could be an asset to the community: to create reciprocal partnerships.

Conducting one-on-one conversations. It is important for the new principal to go to the community and not expect the community to come to the school. Community and labor organizers use one-on-ones as a way to build networks, strengthen relationships, and engage people in their work. A one-on-one conversation is a structured meeting where you share your story with another person and listen to theirs. During the meeting, work to find common ground, listen to concerns, and invite the person to join you to work together on behalf of the community and the school. The more you practice, the better you will get at telling your story. Using one-on-ones is a great way for principals to meet stakeholders and build relationships. It is recommended that principals meet with every staff member, every member of the local school governance board or council, school board or parent groups, leaders in the community (political, business, religious, social service, etc.), and representatives of other stakeholder groups.

Trust the Process. A community school leader must be willing to let the vision and mission of the school bubble up from the grass roots. He or she must trust that everyone in the community wants what is best for children and, if given the opportunity, will choose to be an active participant. Too often, we hear principals complain, "oh well, we invited them but no one showed up." Strong community leaders will use organizing techniques to get people involved. They will call, personally invite (face-to-face), text, and make people feel genuinely needed; they will also use individuals with moral authority in the school community to bring others to the table. Use networks, relationships, and personal invitations to encourage broad participation. Usually people come to meetings because someone asked them or brought them along. Perhaps initial meetings should occur in a neutral location, where people will feel comfortable coming. It is also important to leave one's ego out and know who is the person who has the most credibility, relational trust, or influence to advance an idea or an invitation.

Rediscovering Schools as Assets Within the Community: Create an Asset Map. In keeping with their commitment to building on available assets, community school leaders view partnerships as "two-way streets," with schools giving to the community, as well as receiving support from it. It is helpful to map out all of the assets in a community and create an asset map. Educators and community members can work well together, as individuals or institutions, when they treat each other with respect, take time to build trust, and find ways that their assets can be used to achieve shared goals. It is in this way that schools can serve as the center of community life (Jehl, Blank & McCloud, 2001).

Assets of a Community: Individuals, Associations, and Institutions. Each community boasts a unique combination of assets upon which to build its future. A thorough map of those assets begins with an inventory of the gifts, skills, and capacities of the community's residents. Household by household, building by building, block by block, a vast and often surprising array of individual talents and productive skills can be tapped, few of which are being mobilized for community-building purposes. Asset Mapping should be a part of the school leader's educational training. Too often, leaders are taught to look only at deficits, and this shift in thinking is a critical component of community building. By canvassing the community block by block, a leader can learn who is in the community and what talents they bring and allow stakeholders to know them on a personal level.

Ethics in School Leadership

Given disappointing headlines of a few prominent school officials who be-tray the public trust, school leaders at all levels must be mindful of being ethical and transparent at all times. Unfortunately, a June 2015 Gallup poll of trust in institutions found that only 31 percent of Americans trust public schools.

Political pressure is inherent in the leadership role and is exacerbated by local, state, and national accountability measures to continually improve test scores and satisfy constituents with conflicting agendas, often making every-day decisions into ethical challenges. Clearly, building trust among faculty, staff, students and their families, and the community is integral to a school's improvement efforts; school funding depends upon taxes, and up to 80 per-cent of the public does not have school age children. Raising taxes and passing referenda to support school initiatives in this setting is difficult. Being transparent, welcoming the public, and informing the public as much as possible helps build the public trust.

Educational administration preparation programs are responsible for not only developing preservice educational leaders' awareness of ethical con-cepts and frameworks, but also for developing their ability to apply such concepts and frameworks to make ethical decisions that would positively impact the experiences of students (Vogel, 2002).

Community schools require leaders who are transparent and able to build relational trust among all constituents. Often, community residents have been mistrustful of schools and bureaucracies and many have not had good experi-ences with them. Research shows that social trust among teachers, parents, and school leaders improves much of the routine work of schools and is a key resource for reform (Bryk & Schneider, 2003). Bryk and Schneider (2003) point out that James Comer's School Development project showed that building strong connections between families and school personnel led to improved academic achievement for low-income children (Comer, Haynes, Joyner, and Ben-Avie, 1996) and that Deborah Meier credited building trust among teachers, school leaders, students, and families as key to turning around her school in Harlem (Meier, 2002).

Education is essentially a moral undertaking because it is concerned with the development of human beings; by stepping into educational leadership roles, school and district administrators accept responsibility for the welfare of the students, teachers, and parents that they serve. The values and ethical frameworks that guide leaders become critical to the community they serve and, as students achieve or fail, the larger society. Building credibility and being transparent are two key traits all school leaders must model. A leader must ensure that all decisions are ethical, legal, and of benefit to all children; this is critical to a leader's reputation.

Skills required of educational leaders include strong communication skills, being able to read body language, and being emotionally intelligent. Teachers, families, and other constituents will watch to see if decisions are made in a consistent manner with regard to discipline, how resources are distributed, incidence of students being punished for misbehavior, those referred for special education, and so on, to observe for equity and fairness. They are watching for consistency. Is the leader transparent with regard to the budget? Does the leader become defensive when challenged, or is constructive criticism welcomed? Is the leader trustworthy? Does the principal underpromise and overdeliver (something that delights) or overpromise and underdeliver (something that annoys and breaks trust)? School leaders must walk their talk because everyone is watching them and when they are inconsistent, it betrays that fragile trust that has been established.

Unfortunately, you cannot teach someone to be ethical. But you can teach strategies and behaviors that encourage relational trust. Bryk and Schneider state that relational trust is grounded in the social respect that comes from the social discourse that takes place across the school community. Individuals are continually interpreting the intentions of others within the school community. Their conclusions take into account their previous interactions, the person's reputation, and often commonalities such as race, religion, age, gender, or upbringing. They organize around four themes: respect, personal regard, competence in core role responsibilities, and personal integrity. Principals play a key role in building and sustaining relational trust in a community (2003, 40–45).

This standard also demands that principals are reflective and ensure that all students receive the same opportunities for success. It asks principals to address achievement gaps between demographic subgroups to ensure equal opportunities and equity. Are students of different races and cultural backgrounds treated fairly and equitably with respect to application of discipline, placement in special education, and tracks or honors classes? Ensuring that your institution does not give a disproportionate number of minority students punishment for misconduct, resulting in suspensions and expulsions, is serious business. It requires a great deal of work on the part of the school to ensure that teachers are fair and systems are in place to support interventions to prevent misconduct or academic failure.

Questions to consider include: Are resources dedicated equitably? Are staff hired that represent the community? Are all languages and cultures respected within the school community? Are the leader's words congruent with his or her actions?

To ensure satisfactory responses, a principal needs to create systems and structures that allow for consistency. This means having clear expectations, consequences, supports, and rewards that are understood by all and are implemented with fidelity for all, without regard to subgroup, power status, or politics. Children must be at the center of education, not adults. Effective team members hold each other accountable for their team's success. They will respect children's cultures but will also teach them to live successfully in the mainstream. When holding high expectations for children, a leader must also hold high expectations for all adults in the learning community. For example, if children are expected to be on time, so must adults; if children are expected to dress appropriately, so must adults.

The bottom line is that the school community is always watching. Transparency, clarity, and honesty are imperative. To build a strong community school, a leader must never lose sight of ethics. This extends to email, social media, talks with friends and relatives, and conversations in public places. Remember, if you're comfortable reading about your decisions on the front page of the local newspaper, you can sleep well.

Cultural Competence

The National Policy Board for Educational Administration (NPBEA) now recognizes leadership for equity, social justice, and cultural responsiveness as key components of school leadership. This is something community school leaders have advocated for a very long time as this new standard is critically important to a leader whose mission is to lead the struggle for social justice schooling: building a successful community school where ALL children succeed, regardless of their background, race, economic situation, or zip code. This requires a bold leader who truly is culturally proficient, acts with cultural competence and responsiveness, and makes equity of opportunity essential. Excuses grounded in deficit thinking about students' origins, be they socioeconomic, race, ethnicity, gender, identity, sexual orientation, ableness, or faith—are no longer acceptable (Terrell & Lindsay, 2013).

As our nation's demographics continue to change, principals must gain the knowledge and skills that are required to effectively work with all students, as well as their families and communities, who represent numerous diverse ethnicities, races, cultures, and religions. To do this well, leaders must be able to understand the influence of these and other factors on learning. They also must be aware of and understand patterns of discrimination, inequality, and injustice. Culturally proficient leadership differs from other leadership approaches because "it is anchored in the belief that a leader must clearly understand one's own assumptions, beliefs, and values about people and cultures different from one's self in order to be effective in cross-cultural settings" (Terrell & Lindsay, 2009, p. 5).

Successful community school leaders have to know how to develop culturally responsive schools and help teachers and other staff members build culturally responsive classrooms and school climate. Ladson-Billings (1994) found that culture is central to learning. It plays a role not only in communicating and receiving information, but also in shaping the thinking process of groups and individuals. She notes that pedagogy that acknowledges, responds to, and celebrates fundamental cultures offers full, equitable access to education for students from all cultures.

In addition to leading a culturally competent organization, leaders must become culturally competent themselves. They must also learn how to lead difficult conversations about race, poverty, and stereotypes and confront excuses for achievement gaps. It calls upon them to recognize bilingualism, multiculturalism and diversity as strengths. In order to create a culturally competent school, a leader needs to build his or her ability to have hard conversations about race and class.

The community school principal endeavors to understand the lives of the people he or she serves. This can be accomplished in a number of ways. One important action is to make home visits to understand the world of your students. Home visits help because you learn what resources students have at home, the language of the home, what parents value and their perspective on education, the strengths parents bring to the school community, and their aspirations for their children.

Community school leaders are called upon to have hard conversations about race and equity of opportunity. In order to do this effectively, leaders need to develop strong interpersonal skills and communication skills. It is documented that 80 percent of a principal's day is spent on communication (listening, speaking, reading, and writing). When community members speak different languages, leaders must be sensitive to that fact and have translators available if they do not speak the person's language.

The leader will learn to read body language and understand the nuances that body language may convey in different cultures present in the school community. For example, in one culture, looking a person straight in the eye conveys honesty while in another it may mean disrespect. Understanding what is respectful within cultures and across cultures is imperative, and strong leaders must convey respect in all interactions. It is not just what a person says, but how he or she says it, tone, body language, and actions communicate a message. What is not said can speak volumes.

Leaders will need to build a repertoire of communication strategies and know which is most appropriate to use for different situations. Among the strategies one will need: face-to-face, phone, email, text, individual, group, personal invitations, print media, flyers, church/synagogue/mosque bulletins, and social media. Understanding community expectations, culture, and generational values may serve as a guide, but more than anything, remember that communication, including accessible language (translations) builds relationships.

To be successful at leading a culturally responsive school community, it is not enough for the leader to be culturally competent. He or she must ensure that his faculty, staff, parents, and community stakeholders are also trained and supported in this endeavor. He or she must know how to lead this effort and ensure that the right people are in the organization.

Instructional Leadership

As with all schools, community school principals need to be able to ensure a viable, rigorous curriculum, instructional best practices, and assessment systems that are non-biased and aligned to standards. Marzano (2003) found a "guaranteed and viable curriculum" as the factor having the most impact on student achievement. According to Marzano, this is primarily a combination of "opportunity to learn" and "time." Both have strong correlations with academic achievement, yet they are so interdependent that they constitute one factor.

Because a community school is open longer hours than a traditional school, before school and into the evening, on weekends, and year-round, there is more time to learn, but time must be used well. This requires being strategic in determining what to offer, how to extend the school day and year, and which partners are best able to support school efforts. It also requires monitoring, supporting, and assessing progress to ensure that programs are effective.

All community school principals need to build coherent systems that allow faculty to align rigorous curriculum and assessments to national standards, allow for vertical and horizontal collaboration and planning on the implementation of best practices, for content areas and grade levels. Teachers need common planning time to build common assessments, analyze student work, and conduct data-driven instructional cycles to guide practice and decisions on curriculum and instruction. They also need time to observe one another in practice and provide critical constructive feedback. This does not magically happen; the principal has to understand the vision and need, guide the work and scheduling, monitor the work and delegation of responsibilities, and build capacity on the team.

Differentiated instruction within classrooms is key to meeting the individual needs of every student. Faculty are trained and supported to differentiate instruction and assessment of student learning, including accommodations and modifications for English Language Learners and special education students. In schools with high concentrations of second language learners, it is recommended that all teachers be encouraged to gain ESL or bilingual certification. It is up to community school principals to forge partnerships with universities and other service providers, write proposals and market these ideas to gain buy in from faculty and stakeholders.

Setting up culturally proficient practices within schools is addressed in detail within the new standard. Teachers are supported to create culturally responsive practices and environments for children and families. Boykin and Noguera (2011) found when asset-focused factors are present in the classroom, they are likely to lead to gap-closing outcomes. They can be personal, social, experiential, cultural, and intellectual. When teachers place importance on existing or emerging interests and preferences, motivational inclinations, passions and commitments, attitudes, beliefs, opinions, self-perceptions, personal or collective identities, and prior experiences, knowledge, understandings, skills, and competencies, they build interpersonal relationships, intersubjectivity, and information-processing quality. Interpersonal covers teacher–student relationship quality, teacher expectations, learning goals, and learning collaborations. Intersubjectivity speaks to how well the values, interests, and learning priorities of the teacher are aligned with those of the students and the extent to which these aligned emphases are reflected in the curriculum. Information-processing quality refers to direct and explicit teaching of effective learning, comprehension, and problem-solving strategies that enhance instruction and concept development.

Setting up multitiered systems of support and interventions for children who are not achieving to standards is critical; principals need to know how to ensure implementation and monitoring of these systems of support. Generally, there is not enough staff available to provide the interventions necessary for all children who need help in a school. Creative community school principals engage their partners and bring them in to deliver differentiated supports to students before, during and outside the school day. This requires more coordination, relationship building, fund-raising, and marketing, but enables more resources to flow into the school. In a community school, external partners and community residents may provide additional tutoring and enrichment activities to support student achievement to help every child succeed.

What also distinguishes a community school from other schools is that the community may become the curriculum and a resource to teach the curriculum. In a community school, the curriculum is often tied to the community, and ensuring that it is meaningful, authentic, and relevant is key. Using residents who have lived in the community for a long time as living historians adds depth and enriches learning. Students can also build community asset maps and interview residents about their lives. Service learning projects can enhance the reciprocal nature of the school's partnership with the community and teach students skills and the value of volunteerism, community, and civic duty. Additionally, community partners can support learning outside the school walls and school day as well as throughout the school day as tutors, teachers, or counselors or in any number of roles with training and support.

A community school leader takes seriously the cultural nuances and strengths of residents and community partnerships. Bilingual and multicultural programming, arts, music and culture are embedded into the curriculum. Murals, folkloric dance troupes, jazz ensembles, spoken word, oral history projects, and gospel choirs are but a few examples.

In underresourced communities, ensuring that students have access to technology has been a challenge. The digital divide in poor minority communities remains an issue that community school leaders may address through strategic partnerships, sharing resources and being purposeful in budgeting and grant-writing to stay ahead of the technology curve. By partnering with other agencies, it is easier to write grants and secure additional funding for technology. The technology can also be used to serve adults in the learning community after school hours. Principals ensure that their teachers and staff have the skills, tools, and equipment necessary to integrate technology into lessons and their work. They provide classes for the community residents as well as students and staff on how to use technology tools for life skills. They use technology effectively to communicate with various constituencies and use social media to message excitement about their school curriculum, student learning projects, and accomplishments.

Social-Emotional Support

The expectations and concepts embedded in Standard 5, Community of Care and Support for Students, is one that community school principals have championed for decades. The savvy community school principal will become familiar with the legislative and funding opportunities that can support the school's efforts to develop a community of care for students and families.

On December 10, 2015, President Obama signed into law the Every Student Succeeds Act (ESSA) to replace No Child Left Behind as the primary federal education law. The legislation embraces the whole child, with academic and social supports, wraparound services, and the type of safe, caring environment promoted by the community school movement. One exciting component of the new ESSA is the Full Service Community Schools Program. The Full Service Community Schools Program, provides $6 million in grants to twelve organizations in ten states. It is designed to encourage a coordinated and integrated set of comprehensive academic, social, and health services that respond to the needs of students, their families, and community members. Finding partners involved and/or experienced with a full-service community school program would enhance a principal's support system and his or her community school effort.

It also includes specific language allowing Title 1 funding for integrated student supports that remove academic and nonacademic barriers to student achievement. It enables local educators to access competitive grants to work with integrated student support providers and encourages local communities to utilize evidence-based programs proven to help low-income students succeed in school.

The new ESSA law encourages states to assess students outside the narrow standardized tests that plagued NCLB, and requires schools to use at least one nonacademic indicator such as student and parental engagement, school climate, and school safety. It encourages schools to look at the whole child, something that community schools have always promoted. State and district report cards will address a broad range of indicators such as chronic absence, school climate, safety, rates of suspensions, expulsions, and school-related arrests, and bullying. Since schools do not have the assets or expertise to respond to the challenges of these nonacademic indicators, the ESSA encourages the community school approach by suggesting that schools identify partners. In addition, social-emotional indicators are recognized in the new law. This is an important opportunity for community school principals to build (and fund) wraparound services.

In developing Response to Intervention and Multi-Tiered Systems of Support (MTSS), principals work with teams to create systems that support learners in academics and behavior/social-emotional learning. The interventions can take place before, during, or after school and can be implemented by school personnel or by partners. In a community school, the leader works with other adults in the learning community to set conditions to develop the whole child, focusing on what Dr. James Comer called the developmental pathways (physical, cognitive, social, psychological, language, ethical, and psycho-cultural). One does not have to implement a Comer School Development Program (SDP) model to use these pathways as a guide to building a holistic approach to developmental supports. The school leader needs to understand how these pathways develop in children from birth through young adulthood. A strong community school principal will cultivate the knowledge and skills to build a strong collaborative climate to support the whole child complete with wraparound services and community partnerships.

Another aspect of this holistic process is to develop each student into an active, responsible member of the community. In order to accomplish this, each student must be known, valued, respected, and accountable for his or her actions. As future citizens who are active responsible members of the community, systems are in place to hold them accountable for community service, conduct, events, tech squads, and becoming positive role models for younger children.

Both the principal and the community need to build a strong vision and mission where all adults and students value academic learning and work together to build social and emotional supports for all children to succeed. The principal should be well versed in strategies that promote equity and encourage student voice, participation in student government, restorative justice practices, Positive Behavior Intervention and Supports (PBIS), and other processes that address social and emotional learning and student conduct in a supportive manner that is not punitive. Parent education is an integral component of these approaches because this support must extend to the home and community environment for it to be successful. Being able to motivate parents to become engaged and stay engaged and recruiting the appropriate partners to support their development is a key skill for a community school principal. Many community school principals use opportunities to partner with social services, health providers, pro bono legal aid, day care, and other supports for the child and the entire family, creating a one-stop shop at the school as hub of the community. In addition, various organizations that provide classes in weight loss, exercise, dance, arts, sports, and other types of recreation can become available on-site.

The community school principal needs to make the school a physically and emotionally safe, welcoming place for all cultures and languages represented within the school community. Importantly, those cultures, languages and traditions should be celebrated as strengths and incorporated into the everyday life of the school community. The staff should reflect the community and many members should speak the languages of the community. Translators should be available so that parents and community members feel welcome and included. Murals, dance troupes, literature, assemblies, musical traditions, oral histories, and art forms can be taught by local residents and community partners. Different literature about the school and the website should be available in the languages spoken at the school.

Professional Capacity

This is a new standard which is critical if the principal is going to effectively lead a sustainable learning organization. All too often, great organizations collapse when the "great leader" leaves and capacity has not been developed and succession plans have not been implemented.

A visionary leader will recruit, hire, support, develop, and retain effective and caring faculty and staff aligned with the mission, vision, and core values of the community school. One needs to assess the current staff for strengths and weaknesses, and identify team members who have strong skills and moral authority to create systems, structures, and consistent procedures for recruitment, screening, interviewing, checking references, and hiring. Gaps in staffing must be identified. Once new team members are hired, systems need to be put in place to orient and induct them. Mentors have to be identified and trained; time and funding must be allocated for induction and mentoring. It is estimated that 50 percent of teachers leave the profession within five years, primarily because they are not supported. Therefore, it is vital to support teachers and ensure that they are adequately developed and appreciated.

To prevent turnover and burnout, one has to develop intentional supports and programs to help staff succeed in their work. One way to accomplish this is by developing teacher and staff professional knowledge base, skills, and practice through differentiated opportunities for growth guided by Learning Forward principles of adult learning. By encouraging the work of professional learning communities and effective teams, continuous improvement and collective instructional capacity are expected and supported.

In a community school, the principal develops capacity, opportunities, and support for teacher leadership and also the leadership from other members of the school community through a distributed leadership model. Key skills in building capacity for distributed leadership practice, both within school staff and in the community, include identification of leadership in others, modeling, delegation (knowing what to delegate and what to keep), checking in (how often), monitoring, data analysis, providing real-time, honest feedback, and providing support for success.

Finally, the leader has to model personal and professional health, well-being, and work-life balance, as well as being a continuous learner and reflective practitioner.

In addition to recruiting and building capacity on the faculty and staff, a community school leader has to build capacity across the other organizations that intersect with the school on a daily basis and affect the school's climate and culture. Additionally, care must be taken to work with and nurture talent among the parent and community volunteers as well as partners. This is more important in a community school than in a traditional school.

Professional Learning Communities

The research on professional learning communities shows the strong effect of providing workplace conditions that foster continuous professional development to improve outcomes for every child. This happens when teachers and staff take collective responsibility for the academic, social, emotional, and physical needs of each student aligned to the mission, vision, and core values of the school. In a community school, the leader should also expand this practice to involve both formal partners and other stakeholders.

In order for professional learning community to be effective, principals have to be skilled in implementing the concepts. A great deal of planning and pre-organization goes into this process. A principal would have to identify key team members to be trained initially to observe a high-functioning PLC in operation. They in turn would train members of the school community team. There would be reading, professional development, scheduling, allocation of funding, skill building in data-driven decision-making, providing nonjudgmental feedback, organizing agendas, minutes, team development, and so on. This is a multiyear process and one must be prepared for the long haul.

Additional professional development will need to be implemented to encourage peer observations of practice in real time or video, providing feedback, and examination of student work. Resources and programs will be aligned to meet the social, emotional, and physical needs of each student. The principal will know how to lead the faculty to engage in quality review of their practice (to hold up the mirror) on a continuous improvement cycle.

Some important skills a principal must possess and be able to lead are: data inquiry cycles, walk-throughs, peer observations, providing feedback, critical friend groups, study groups, data summits, and so on. The principal must understand and be able to lead teams, team development, and team accountability.

As new members of the faculty and staff are hired, careful induction and mentoring programs need to be developed and implemented to ensure that staff know expectations, understand their jobs, and are supported to be successful. Without adequate support, teachers and other school personnel burn out and leave the profession within a few years. This has a negative impact on the school, the community, and its learners. Building capacity and a strong accountability team is a major task of the school leader.

Family and Community Engagement

In a 2005 report published by the Education Commission of the States, many principals reported that formal preparation programs taught them little about how or even why to engage with families and communities as partners. Principals cited the importance of substantive, community-focused content and hands-on experience. They suggested a need for training in political skill-building, communication strategies, collaboration techniques, exposure to negotiation techniques, relevant data and analysis methods, and work on adult development. They suggested that these topics be embedded in field-based practice and be taught by interdisciplinary practitioners from education, business, law, public policy, communication, and social work. Additionally, work on shared leadership and team-building would be helpful. The 2015 standards for school leaders underscore the need for meaningful and reciprocal engagement with families and community. Therefore, these needs are even more critical today.

Given the findings above, aspiring principals would benefit from experiences embedded in their training programs that expose them to work with immigrant and disenfranchised communities to gain a fundamental understanding of issues of race, poverty, immigration, housing, and language diversity. By having experiences working in community-based organizations, candidates can gain exposure and sensitivity to help them engage with fami-

lies, community members, and various partners. By becoming knowledgeable about research-based models of parent engagement, they will be able to
support teachers and staff to work more effectively with families and community members on behalf of students.

Working in community schools is inherently political. Most school leaders receive little or no training in political skills development, and are often
unprepared for the challenges they face when the answers aren't in the book.
Trial and error is a great teacher, but it can be costly. Principal preparation
programs do not typically help candidates develop political skills (Winton &
Pollack, 2013). How principals act politically impacts teaching, learning,
change efforts, school governance, relationships, and democracy in education (Blasé and Anderson, 1995; Blasé & Blasé, 2002b; Malen & Ogwawa,
1988; Ryan, 2010 cited in Winton & Pollack, 2013).

Operations and Management

To collaborate effectively with multiple organizations, one must ensure that
all partners are on board with the shared community school mission and
vision, and are willing to work hand in hand to achieve it. Managing human
and financial resources from different organizations and funders requires a
great deal of planning, report generation, bookkeeping, and accountability. A
key area is to develop systems and structures to support operational excellence and management. Using technology effectively to manage systems,
monitor, gather data, disseminate information to stakeholders, and store data
requires a vision, a budget, training, and expertise. Managing relationships
between partners, community stakeholders, school board, central office, and
feeder and connecting schools is a key part of the leader's job. As a manager
and leader, one must understand the laws, school code, board policies, and
continued practice expectations. A leader must develop accountability feedback loops to ensure compliance with laws, contracts, and grants. If waivers
are needed because of an innovative practice the community is implementing, the leader needs to ensure that proper channels and procedures are followed so that the projects are not derailed for noncompliance of a regulation.
For example, if partners use the building space, are all school board policies
followed to provide or "rent" space, use the facilities, and ensure insurance
documents are on file, even if no charge is levied?

Due to the complexities of coordination, many community schools have a
coordinator who aligns the work of school and community partners and
aligns programs with the goals of the school (Blank, Berg & Melaville 2006).
While this is potentially quite helpful, it can also create complexities for the
principal if the coordinator actually works for another organization and is not
directly supervised by the principal. When this situation occurs, it is critical
for the coordinator's supervisor and the principal to work hand in hand so

there is no conflict and the coordinator understands the expectations of the principal are one and the same as the expectations of the community-based organization. Having structures and policies in place to deal with conflict is helpful, especially in a community school where multiple organizations operate, many with competing agendas. By building consensus around ground rules and standard operating procedures, many conflicts can be avoided. When conflict does occur, having a solid process in place serves as a guide. Consistent implementation of the process will result in the perception of fairness.

By assessing the needs of students and strengths of faculty and staff, the principal is able to determine the best way to assign roles and responsibilities to maximize student learning. Having procedures in place that protect against interruptions of learning time results in more time on task and improved learning. When classrooms are used for different purposes before or after school hours, the team must develop policies and procedures to ensure that the space is used respectfully and that there are consequences for not leaving the space ready for instruction the next day. Are the appropriate constituents included (e.g., teachers, parents and community partners) on the planning committees so that their needs and expectations are considered when drafting these policies and procedures?

Blank, Berg, and Melaville (2006) underscore the importance of building an infrastructure to support change within and across systems. Developing and maintaining data and communication systems for stakeholders to access pertinent real-time data supports school improvement efforts and collaboration. The community school principal has to think systemically and embed the vision and mission in all work. By creating a strong infrastructure of support, the community school's vision can be embedded through its partner organizations and across the community. The leader's success hinges on being able to work productively across systems, to advance the agenda, facilitate data collection and evaluation across organizations, and develop sound public engagement and implementation strategies. The leader needs to be able to provide necessary technical assistance and professional development to stakeholders and partners. The leader must be able to connect with individuals inside the school, inside the district but external to the school, and also with families, community residents, businesses, and others external to the school.

The community school leader needs to develop a plan to fund the community school for multiple years. Strategic planning, communication, and continuous evaluation are needed. The principal should know how to set SMART goals, monitor progress toward goals, and communicate results to multiple constituencies and funders. Once everything is put in place, it is vital to ensure that the programs can become institutionalized, which means putting together funding for the long term. Community schools need a multiple-year, diversified base of support. Leaders of successful initiatives find resources from local, state, federal, and private sources and are able to redirect services and personnel from partner agencies. Leaders must collaborate to develop additional funding streams so that initiatives don't die when a grant ends. Innovative leaders look across institutions to see where different initiatives can be funded. For example, if a partner can provide a social worker, then the school can use that funding for other needs. When the entire community is engaged, the various initiatives are more visible. Funders like to invest in initiatives that use resources wisely, and they like to invest in organizations that understand how to leverage their funds to stretch them further. A community school leader should be continually looking for new sources of revenue and use networking skills to market their programs to those who can assist.

Financing a community school effort is more complex than budgeting for a school. While it is more complex, the opportunities for expanded financing and shared resources are increased. Once a good infrastructure is built with solid agreements and memos of understanding in place, an entrepreneurial leader can build a community hub that is funded from multiple sources beyond the school system. Often public/private partnerships or leveraged partnerships help fund projects that a single entity could not qualify for on its own. Funders generally want to see that the dollars they invest have a greater impact and by having several organizations work together, they can leverage funding and maximize impact.

Among the skills and areas of expertise a leader needs, the first will be to understand the laws, policies, and regulations governing all money streams that come into the school. Gaining skill in fund-raising, grantwriting, philanthropy, entrepreneurship, and building two-way-partnerships is of paramount importance. Writing one-page white papers that describe their concept or idea is very helpful. Also, many funders appreciate simple bullet point descriptions. When meeting with potential funders, leaders should know how to listen to what the funder is interested in, learn how to frame the "ask," how to close the deal, and to find common ground. He or she also needs to develop others who can do this, but it is vitally important for the leader.

School Improvement

The final standard, School Improvement, calls on educators to make school more effective for each student, teachers and staff, families, and the community promote each student's academic success and well-being. By adopting a continuous improvement perspective to achieve the vision, fulfill the mission, and promote the core values of the school, they will support the academic success and well-being of each student. To do so effectively, educators must engage in data-driven decision making as a complement to research-based practice. This requires an emphasis on goal setting, measurement, and feedback loops so that they can reflect on their programs and process, relate them to student outcomes, and make refinements suggested by the outcome data so that faculty, staff, families, and community members will rally behind a shared vision and mission for improvement. Building mutual commitment and accountability as well as capacity for success is critical.

Principals must know how to gather the data and present it to stakeholders in simple, easy-to-follow displays that paint a true picture of the organization, its strengths, and areas for growth. The principal has to be able to establish a sense of urgency among stakeholders to get them to buy into the improvement effort and must engage others in an ongoing process of evidence-based inquiry, data analysis, strategic goal setting, planning, implementation, and evaluation.

CONCLUDING THOUGHTS

Leading a community school takes a special kind of leader, one with an entrepreneurial spirit and strong commitment to equity and social justice. Moreover, he or she must find joy in endless work with people and processes. To successfully lead a school that prepares students for our future world, the community school leader must know more than curriculum, instruction, and assessment strategies. To successfully develop a school where *all* children succeed, regardless of background, race, religion, economic situation, or zip code, the leader must master all of the knowledge, skills, and dispositions that a principal of a traditional school does, augmented by more developed skills and dispositions in a number of key areas. The new Standards for Educational Leaders 2015 and the dispositions of transformational leaders noted in this chapter are a great starting point for anyone wanting to lead a strong community school effort. Special attention and more development are needed in important areas related to working effectively with parents and community, sharing power, political training, financing community schools, working with community-based organizations, conflict management, marketing, using data to tell stories, fund-raising and grantwriting, networking, building multilevel infrastructure, systems thinking, diversity training, and cultural competence. Anyone contemplating community school leadership should go through the 2015 leadership standards and the areas listed above to create a personal professional development plan. It is imperative that universities, community-based organizations, and districts develop and support community school leaders. They are best served by bringing together an interdisciplinary team that includes experienced community school leaders to redesign programs and develop a project-based approach that also integrates community-based internships.

PROFESSIONAL STANDARDS FOR EDUCATIONAL LEADERS 2015

STANDARD 1. MISSION, VISION, AND CORE VALUES

Effective educational leaders develop, advocate, and enact a shared mission, vision, and core values of high-quality education and academic success and well-being of each student.

Effective leaders:

a. Develop an educational mission for the school to promote the academic success and well-being of each student.
b. In collaboration with members of the school and the community and using relevant data, develop and promote a vision for the school on the successful learning and development of each child and on instructional and organizational practices that promote such success.
c. Articulate, advocate, and cultivate core values that define the school's culture and stress the imperative of child-centered education; high expectations and student support; equity, inclusiveness, and social justice; openness, caring, and trust; and continuous improvement.
d. Strategically develop, implement, and evaluate actions to achieve the vision for the school.
e. Review the school's mission and vision and adjust them to changing expectations and opportunities for the school, and changing needs and situations of students.
f. Develop shared understanding of and commitment to mission, vision, and core values within the school and the community.
g. Model and pursue the school's mission, vision, and core values in all aspects of leadership.

STANDARD 2. ETHICS AND PROFESSIONAL NORMS

Effective educational leaders act ethically and according to professional norms to promote each student's academic success and well-being.

Effective leaders:

a. Act ethically and professionally in personal conduct, relationships with others, decision-making, stewardship of the school's resources, and all aspects of school leadership.

b. Act according to and promote the professional norms of integrity, fairness, transparency, trust, collaboration, perseverance, learning, and continuous improvement.

c. Place children at the center of education and accept responsibility for each student's academic success and well-being.

d. Safeguard and promote the values of democracy, individual freedom and responsibility, equity, social justice, community, and diversity.

e. Lead with interpersonal and communication skill, social-emotional insight, and understanding of all students' and staff members' backgrounds and cultures.

f. Provide moral direction for the school and promote ethical and professional behavior among faculty and staff.

STANDARD 3. EQUITY AND CULTURAL RESPONSIVENESS

Effective educational leaders strive for equity of educational opportunity and culturally responsive practices to promote each student's academic success and well-being.

Effective leaders:

a. Ensure that each student is treated fairly, respectfully, and with an understanding of each student's culture and context.

b. Recognize, respect, and employ each student's strengths, diversity, and culture as assets for teaching and learning.

c. Ensure that each student has equitable access to effective teachers, learning opportunities, academic and social support, and other resources necessary for success.

d. Develop student policies and address student misconduct in a positive, fair, and unbiased manner.

e. Confront and alter institutional biases of student marginalization, deficit-based schooling, and low expectations associated with race, class, culture and language, gender and sexual orientation, and disability or special status.

f. Promote the preparation of students to live productively in and contribute to the diverse cultural contexts of a global society.

g. Act with cultural competence and responsiveness in their interactions, decision making, and practice.

h. Address matters of equity and cultural responsiveness in all aspects of leadership.

STANDARD 4. CURRICULUM, INSTRUCTION, AND ASSESSMENT

Effective educational leaders develop and support intellectually rigorous and coherent systems of curriculum, instruction, and assessment to promote each student's academic success and well-being.

Effective leaders:

a. Implement coherent systems of curriculum, instruction, and assessment that promote the mission, vision, and core values of the school, embody high expectations for student learning, align with academic standards, and are culturally responsive.
b. Align and focus systems of curriculum, instruction, and assessment within and across grade levels to promote student academic success, love of learning, the identities and habits of learners, and healthy sense of self.
c. Promote instructional practice that is consistent with knowledge of child learning and development, effective pedagogy, and the needs of each student.
d. Ensure instructional practice that is intellectually challenging, authentic to student experiences, recognizes student strengths, and is differentiated and personalized.
e. Promote the effective use of technology in the service of teaching and learning.
f. Employ valid assessments that are consistent with knowledge of child learning and development and technical standards of measurement.

STANDARD 5. COMMUNITY OF CARE AND SUPPORT FOR STUDENTS

Effective educational leaders cultivate an inclusive, caring, and supportive school community that promotes the academic success and well-being of each student.

Effective leaders:

a. Build and maintain a safe, caring, and healthy school environment that meets the academic, social, emotional, and physical needs of each student.
b. Create and sustain a school environment in which each student is known, accepted and valued, trusted and respected, cared for, and encouraged to be an active and responsible member of the school community.

   c. Provide coherent systems of academic and social supports, services, extracurricular activities, and accommodations to meet the range of learning needs of each student.

   d. Promote adult-student, student-peer, and school-community relationships that value and support academic learning and positive social and emotional development.

   e. Cultivate and reinforce student engagement in school and positive student conduct.

   f. Infuse the school's learning environment with the cultures and languages of the school's community.

STANDARD 6. PROFESSIONAL CAPACITY OF SCHOOL PERSONNEL

Effective educational leaders develop the professional capacity and practice of school personnel to promote each student's academic success and well-being.

Effective leaders:

   a. Recruit, hire, support, develop, and retain effective and caring teachers and other professional staff and form them into an educationally effective faculty.

   b. Plan for and manage staff turnover and succession, providing opportunities for effective induction and mentoring of new personnel.

   c. Develop teachers' and staff members' professional knowledge, skills, and practice through differentiated opportunities for learning and growth, guided by understanding of professional and adult learning and development.

   d. Foster continuous improvement of individual and collective instructional capacity to achieve outcomes envisioned for each student.

   e. Deliver actionable feedback about instruction and other professional practice through valid, research-anchored systems of supervision and evaluation to support the development of teachers' and staff members' knowledge, skills, and practice.

   f. Empower and motivate teachers and staff to the highest levels of professional practice and to continuous learning and improvement.

   g. Develop the capacity, opportunities, and support for teacher leadership and leadership from other members of the school community.

   h. Promote personal and professional health, well-being, and work-life balance

   i. Tend to their own learning and effectiveness through reflection, study, and improvement, maintaining a healthy work-life balance.

STANDARD 7. PROFESSIONAL COMMUNITY FOR TEACHERS AND STAFF

Effective educational leaders foster a professional community of teachers and other professional staff to promote each student's academic success and well-being.

Effective leaders:

a. Develop workplace conditions for teachers and other professional staff that promote effective professional development, practice, and student learning.
b. Empower and entrust teachers and staff with collective responsibility for meeting the academic, social, emotional, and physical needs of each student, pursuant to the mission, vision, and core values of the school.
c. Establish and sustain a professional culture of engagement and commitment to shared vision, goals, and objectives pertaining to the education of the whole child; high expectations for professional work; ethical and equitable practice; trust and open communication; collaboration, collective efficacy, and continuous individual and organizational learning and improvement.
d. Promote mutual accountability among teachers and other professional staff for each student's success and the effectiveness of the school as a whole.
e. Develop and support open, productive, caring, and trusting working relationships among leaders, faculty, and staff to promote professional capacity and the improvement of practice.
f. Design and implement job-embedded and other opportunities for professional learning collaboratively with faculty and staff.
g. Provide opportunities for collaborative examination of practice, collegial feedback, and collective learning.
h. Encourage faculty-initiated improvement of programs and practices.

STANDARD 8. MEANINGFUL ENGAGEMENT OF FAMILIES AND COMMUNITY

Effective educational leaders engage families and the community in meaningful, reciprocal, and mutually beneficial ways to promote each student's academic success and well-being.

Effective leaders:

a. Are approachable, accessible, and welcoming to families and members of the community.
b. Create and sustain positive, collaborative, and productive relationships with families and the community for the benefit of students.
c. Engage in regular and open two-way communication with families and the community about the school, students, needs, problems, and accomplishments.
d. Maintain a presence in the community to understand its strengths and needs, develop productive relationships, and engage its resources for the school.
e. Create means for the school community to partner with families to support student learning in and out of school.
f. Understand, value, and employ the community's cultural, social, intellectual, and political resources to promote student learning and school improvement.
g. Develop and provide the school as a resource for families and the community.
h. Advocate for the school and district, and for the importance of education and student needs and priorities to families and the community
i. Advocate publicly for the needs and priorities of students, families, and the community.
j. Build and sustain productive partnerships with public and private sectors to promote school improvement and student learning.

STANDARD 9. OPERATIONS AND MANAGEMENT

Effective educational leaders manage school operations and resources to promote each student's academic success and well-being.

Effective leaders:

a. Institute, manage, and monitor operations and administrative systems that promote the mission and vision of the school.
b. Strategically manage staff resources, assigning and scheduling teachers and staff to roles and responsibilities that optimize their professional capacity to address each student's learning needs.
c. Seek, acquire, and manage fiscal, physical, and other resources to support curriculum, instruction, and assessment; student learning community; professional capacity and community; and family and community engagement.
d. Are responsible, ethical, and accountable stewards of the school's monetary and nonmonetary resources, engaging in effective budgeting and accounting practices.

   e. Protect teachers' and other staff members' work and learning from disruption.

   f. Employ technology to improve the quality and efficiency of operations and management.

   g. Develop and maintain data and communication systems to deliver actionable information for classroom and school improvement.

   h. Know, comply with, and help the school community understand local, state, and federal laws, rights, policies, and regulations so as to promote student success.

   i. Develop and manage relationships with feeder and connecting schools for enrollment management and curricular and instructional articulation.

   j. Develop and manage productive relationships with the central office and school board.

   k. Develop and administer systems for fair and equitable management of conflict among students, faculty and staff, leaders, families, and community.

   l. Manage governance processes and internal and external politics toward achieving the school's mission and vision.

STANDARD 10. SCHOOL IMPROVEMENT

Effective educational leaders act as agents of continuous improvement to promote each student's academic success and well-being.

Effective leaders:

   a. Seek to make school more effective for each student, teachers and staff, families, and the community.

   b. Use methods of continuous improvement to achieve the vision, fulfill the mission, and promote the core values of the school.

   c. Prepare the school and the community for improvement, promoting readiness, an imperative for improvement, instilling mutual commitment and accountability, and developing the knowledge, skills, and motivation to succeed in improvement.

   d. Engage others in an ongoing process of evidence-based inquiry, learning, strategic goal setting, planning, implementation, and evaluation for continuous school and classroom improvement.

   e. Employ situationally appropriate strategies for improvement, including transformational and incremental, adaptive approaches and attention to different phases of implementation.

f. Assess and develop the capacity of staff to assess the value and applicability of emerging educational trends and the findings of research for the school and its improvement.

g. Develop technically appropriate systems of data collection, management, analysis, and use, connecting as needed to the district office and external partners for support in planning, implementation, monitoring, feedback, and evaluation.

h. Adopt a systems perspective and promote coherence among improvement efforts and all aspects of school organization, programs, and service.

i. Manage uncertainty, risk, competing initiatives, and politics of change with courage and perseverance, providing support and encouragement, and openly communicating the need for, process for, and outcomes of improvement efforts.

j. Develop and promote leadership among teachers and staff for inquiry, experimentation and innovation, and initiating and implementing improvement.

Chapter Nine

Evaluating Community School Leadership

Adeline Ray, Daniel Diehl, and Neil Naftzger

The simplest definition of what community schooling "looks like" may be to think of a community center where children are educated and the community gathers to socialize and learn:

> A survey of new schools in over 20 leading cities demonstrates the drive to provide buildings that can be used by adults as well as children, converting modern schools into centers that meet new educational demands . . . thinking of schools where opportunities are provided during the summer and long winter evenings for young people's educational and recreational needs, as well as a place with evening classes, space for parents to meet and for public lectures. (Perry, 1912)

Present-day community schooling in Chicago was born when leaders from philanthropy, the Chicago Public Schools (CPS), and a myriad of social service, advocacy, and community-based organizations worked together to make Chicago home to one of the largest systems of community schools in the country. Drawing on the strength of the city's diverse neighborhoods and numerous community-based organizations, the Community Schools Initiative (CSI) at the Chicago Public Schools has made implementation of the community school strategy a critical element of school improvement and community revitalization efforts.

Since 2002, the initiative has inaugurated the Community School strategy in over 250 schools. The strategy develops schools as central, neighborhood locations where students receive an education and schools work with community groups to connect children and families to a range of services that foster individual and economic well-being. These schools are open extended hours, in use up to seven days a week year-round, creating a vibrant community meeting place, drawing together a range of resources that support the academic, health, and social service needs of students and their families.

> *Where schools truly become the centers of the community, great things happen. . . . We need the schools open much longer hours, and we don't have to do this all ourselves . . . you can bring in great nonprofits, mentoring and tutoring groups to co-locate their services and bolster the community from the school.*
> (Arne Duncan, U. S. Secretary of Education, to Charlie Rose, March 13, 2009)

Mobilizing the resources and expertise of communities to remove barriers to learning and enrich and expand the breadth of each child's experiences is a clear statement of belief that education goes way beyond the closed system of a school comprised of teachers and students in classrooms. In community schools, education is a communal and collective endeavor.

Early evaluations of community schools in Chicago demonstrated that implementing this community-focused strategy improved the climate for learning for all students. Schools were able to close the achievement gap in reading, math, and science. Working with community partners, these school leaders instituted early interventions that kept student disciplinary infractions from escalating. Additionally, these schools showed improved attendance and reduced mobility (Whalen, 2002, 2007).

These third-party evaluations of community schools in Chicago also disclosed the indispensible role principals play in advancing the strategy. In addition to reaching out into the community to engage families and develop new resources for the school, community-focused principals actively work with school personnel to make sure critical building services continue beyond regular school hours into the evening and weekends in support of community members' access to school facilities (Whalen, 2002, 2007).

Thorough research conducted by the Consortium on Chicago School Research demonstrates the importance of the principal in driving school improvement (Sebring & Bryk, 2000; Bryk, et al., 2010). Indeed, the Children's Aid Society (CAS, 2011) and the Coalition for Community Schools (Blank, et al., 2003), national leaders in the community school movement, stress the importance of principal support and engagement in developing and sustaining a community school.

Because community schooling is a strategy for whole school improvement, it is not surprising then that a talented and supportive principal is fundamental to the success of the community school. It is the community-focused leadership of the community school principal that drives the attraction of resources to the school, engages the local community, and involves parents in a most meaningful way. The CSI Implementation and Sustainability Process Strategy (ISPS), a framework for implementing the community school strategy in building partnerships and assessing the school needs while building a sustainable Community School, evidences this.

In the research-based CSI evaluation to determine the ISPS framework that contributes to successful implementation and sustainability of the CPS community school strategy, the CSI evaluation team identified "Principal Commits to the Community School Model" as the first step (Figure 9.1) in transforming to a community-focused school.

This first, critical step represents that the principal:

- Has reflected upon, understands and believes in the value of the Community School model as a framework for school-wide improvement and change.
- Has fully committed to engage in a mutually beneficial collaboration with the Lead Partner Agency (LPA) and community members.
- Is committed to community schooling through their actions, policies, and relationships with stakeholders (Zander, et al., 2011).

Measuring those actions, policies, and relationships for community-focused leaders is critical to yield the positive results they want to realize for their students, families, and community members.

A central tenet of community schools is alignment of programs, services, and operations of the school with unique community needs and assets. As such, it is understood that strategies designed to build on assets and address needs must allow for a degree of adaptability to be effective. This tenet poses a challenge to evaluating community schools.

When drawing conclusions from evaluation studies, it is paramount that interventions include a focus on the processes used to generate results. Simply stated, if we see positive or negative outcomes from an intervention, we would want to know what led to these outcomes. Therefore, since school communities are unique and community schools by definition are designed to build on local assets and address local needs, evaluation of community schools must first seek to operationalize the interventions that are aligned with targeted outcomes.

As described previously, the *CSI Implementation and Sustainability Process Strategy* (ISPS) provides a framework for implementing community schools. The framework outlines core operational features and processes common across schools, while allowing flexibility to build on unique assets and address community school needs. In doing so, the framework provides schools with a road map for implementation, allowing documentation of a process to both inform implementation and assess outcomes. An overview of the process used to guide implementation with a focus on measuring community-focused leadership follows.

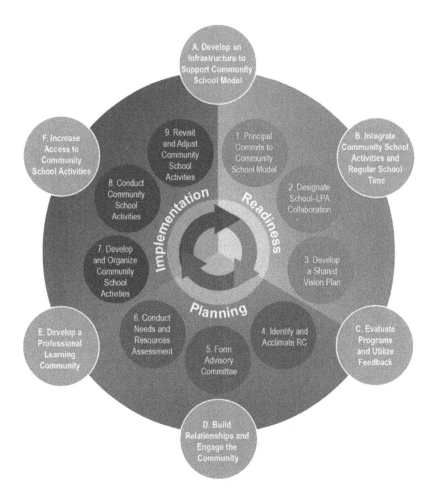

Figure 9.1.   Principal Commits to the Community School Model. Source: Community Schools Initiative Implementation Framework. Reprinted from *Chicago
public schools community schools initiative 2011–12 impact evaluation brief,* by
Chicago Public Schools and American Institutes for Research. (2014, Novem-
ber). Copyright © Chicago Public Schools and American Institutes for Research.
Reprinted with permission.

OVERVIEW OF THE CPS CSI CONTINUOUS QUALITY
IMPROVEMENT PROCESS

Grounded in the ISPS framework, the CSI developed a Continuous Quality
Improvement Process (CQIP) as a means of (a) documenting implementation
across schools, (b) providing schools a process to assess areas that are going
well and potential areas for improvement, and (c) identifying action steps to

strengthen implementation. The CQIP is grounded in the belief that high-quality community schools are no accident. Instead, high-quality community schools are the result of intentional processes for assessment of assets and needs, leading to action plans in response to findings from these assessments.

The process involves assessment of two key dimensions of community school implementation: (a) the organizational or school-level and (b) the point-of-service (activity) level. The organizational or school level assessment is characterized by the operations and structure of the organization or school (e.g., how advisory committees are structured, commitment of school and community leaders to the process), while the point-of-service assessment is characterized by participant interactions and attributes of direct service (e.g., student and adult engagement in programs and services, interactions among participants and staff).

A comprehensive User Guide was developed to support the process. This guide includes key implementation phases and tasks, organizational and point-of-service assessment tools, and action planning worksheets. An overview of this process is first provided, followed by a discussion of assessment tools in the context of community-focused leadership.

KEY IMPLEMENTATION PHASES AND TASKS (PROCESS)

Identifying the quality improvement facilitator. As a first step, the school designates a Quality Improvement Facilitator. This person is responsible for coordinating the CQIP assessment team who will inform the process, schedule meetings, and complete forms on time and in partnership with the assessment team. Importantly, the school has flexibility in designating the individual best suited for the position.

Determining the quality improvement assessment phase. Once the facilitator is determined, the next step is to identify which quality improvement process phase and respective tasks the school should begin their work. Implementation of the quality improvement process is divided into school year time phases. Schools new to the Quality Improvement Process would *typically* begin with Phase 1 tasks (described below) and initiate the process at the beginning of the school year. Schools that have prior experience with community schooling and the CQIP may begin with either Phase 2 or Phase 3 (described below). The primary goal of each main phase is the creation and implementation of an action plan of improvement. The action plan identifies key findings from school- or organizational-level and point-of-service assessments. These findings are used to inform specific objectives for the year and actions that will be taken to realize the objectives. The annual process of completing the action plan is viewed as an essential principle of the CSI Continuous Quality Improvement Process.

Assessing readiness. When determining the best entry point into the implementation phase, a school is first encouraged to assess readiness to engage in the process. This differentiated practice allows a school unfamiliar with the process to start at a beginning level of assessment and review, while a school that is further down the road in implementation may build on prior work. Importantly, this decision is not driven by the length of time that a school has been implementing community schooling. Instead, the appropriate beginning phase is determined by a school's history of organizational and point-of-service quality assessment and its ability to develop and effectively implement action plans based on those assessments. During this step, the facilitator is encouraged to consult with CSI leadership while exploring the following questions: (a) Have you developed a Quality Improvement Assessment Team that is dedicated to assessing quality of your community school? (b) Have you previously assessed organizational quality using the organizational assessments? (c) Have you assessed point-of-service quality using point-of-service assessments? (d) Have you developed and begun to implement an annual action plan?

Orientation to the continuous quality improvement process. Once the implementation phase is determined, schools participate in a community schools orientation conducted by CSI leadership and partners. This orientation includes guidance for conducting the CSI Continuous Quality Improvement Process. Schools then plan for implementation of the process, beginning with the phase determined from the readiness assessment. Specific phases and related tasks of each phase are described in more detail below.

Phase One. This phase involves assessment of the first two domains associated with organizational or school-level functioning (Domains 1 and 2). To support this process, a series of rubrics were developed that allow a school to self-assess establishment of the community school structure, resources, and programming. A key task in this phase involves the creation of a Quality Improvement Assessment Team (assessment team). This is a dedicated team within the community school that is responsible for supporting the Quality Improvement Process. Team members are responsible for attending all meetings and actively participating in assessment and action-planning processes. Importantly, the community school decides the best composition of this team. This may be a new team within the school developed for this purpose, or it may be incorporated as an added responsibility of an existing community school structure (e.g., a subset of the full Community School Advisory Committee). Results of the assessment are used by the assessment team to inform the action plan.

Phase Two. This phase involves assessment of the last two rubric domains associated with organizational or school-level functioning (Domain 3 and 4). The rubrics associated with these domains include a focus on continuous improvement and sustainability of program, services, and infrastructure.

Additionally, during this phase, the school also completes a point-of-service quality assessment. While the rubric assessment is conducted at the assessment team level, the point-of-service assessment is conducted by trained observers who are directly observing programs and services operating at the school site. Results of both assessments are used by the assessment team to inform the action plan.

Phase Three. During this phase, the school's assessment team selects specific areas of focus and assessment based on past progress and current needs. It is expected that this continued assessment applies at least one domain from the rubrics and one administration of the point-of-service assessment. Once again, results of both assessments are used by the assessment team to guide action planning in this phase.

In sum, the CQIP provides a comprehensive framework for collecting information related to the implementation of a community school strategy. The framework incorporates specific assessment tools that allow for both organizational and point-of-service quality assessment. The framework encourages school and community stakeholders to engage in this self-assessment, collaboratively working to identify areas of strength and improvement through the development of action plans.

ASSESSING COMMUNITY-FOCUSED LEADERSHIP

Community-focused leadership is demonstrated through high-functioning collaborative partnerships among schools and communities that demonstrate shared vision and commitment. Structures are created that support this level of integration, including high-functioning advisory committees, formalized needs and asset assessments, and programs and services that are high quality and responsive to the uniqueness of the school community. Specific aspects of the CSI CQIP Self-Assessment Rubric are reviewed below to illustrate assessment of community-focused leadership.

As mentioned above, the CPS CSI evaluation team developed a series of rubrics to assess organizational and school-level functioning. The tool is divided into four core domains of implementation:

- Domain 1 is focused on establishing and maintaining essential structures and resources needed for an effective community school.
- Domain 2 includes a focus on establishing and maintaining community school programs and services.
- Domain 3 focuses on establishing and maintaining continuous improvement structures.

- Domain 4 focuses on the development of strategies and identification of commitments to secure resources to financially and organizationally sustain the community school.

Each domain includes operational elements and sub-elements that are used to further define implementation. Guiding questions are included to encourage discussion of the sub-element and generate one of the following ratings: 1—planning, 2—emerging, 3—proficient, and 4—exemplary. Under each of the response choices, observable criteria are included as a description of implementation relative to each of the possible ratings.

Across all four rubric domains, there are a total of nineteen elements and fifty sub-elements. Collectively, the criteria being assessed provide the school with a comprehensive understanding of various facets of implementation. To illustrate measurement of community-focused leadership specifically, selected sub-elements and exemplary criteria used to define the construct are presented below under each of the four rubric domains associated with organizational and school-level assessment. These examples provide the reader with an understanding of what community-focused leadership may look like within a community school.

DOMAIN 1. Establish and maintain essential structures and resources needed for an effective community school.

Shared commitment among partners to the community school model. A shared commitment to implementing the community school model is evident among various school and community stakeholders. This commitment is evident in how school leaders, staff, and community partners communicate about and plan their work. Given the level of commitment among partners, the model is not in jeopardy of leadership changes at the school or community partner level.

Shared understanding of the community school model. A shared understanding among stakeholders is created whereby partners understand that the work goes beyond a narrow focus on academic achievement and test performance and instead includes a broader focus on the well-being of students, families, and community members. This is reflected in the shared identification and of work toward outcomes that are associated with academic performance, student well-being (e.g., measures of social emotional learning, student engagement in different types of learning opportunities) and family well-being (e.g., family measures related to employment, education, and parenting). Further, the model is considered to be a framework for school-wide improvement and change. This is demonstrated by strategies that are clearly connected to school improvement goals, as documented in the school improvement plan for this school or other sources.

Advisory committee established with diverse representation. Composition of and attendance by the advisory committee have been set. An advisory committee including community members, students, and other key school and community stakeholders is developed to guide the work of the community school. Members consistently attend regularly scheduled meetings, and all members understand and can articulate the core purpose of and their role on the committee.

Development of a shared vision. A shared vision among stakeholders for the community school is jointly created by the school and community partner, while including substantial input from various internal and external stakeholder groups (e.g., community partners, community members, parents, students, teachers, school staff, building administration, district administration, advisory committee). The type of information used to inform the shared vision includes personal experiences, informal feedback from other stakeholders, a review of existing data sources, and newly collected data for the purpose of creating a shared vision among stakeholders for the community school.

Collaborative goal setting aligned within the vision and mission. Formal goals for the community school have been developed. Beyond engaging in an intentional process of collaboratively identifying goals for the partnership, goals reflect an integration of the mission/vision of both the school and community partner. Evidence for this integration includes (a) The written goals for the community school are clearly aligned with the vision/mission of both the school and the community partner, and (b) goals are reviewed and updated annually by the partnership to ensure that they are based on current need.

Collaborative decision-making. The decision-making process is *clearly shared* whereby the school and community partner are both involved in making decisions related to (a) types of service, (b) staff selection, (c) scheduling, (d) participant recruitment, and (e) funding.

Final decisions almost always involve input from both the school and community partner. In addition to lead community partners, other community partners play a role in this process. Further, key aspects of service delivery are reviewed at least annually by the school and community partners, and an advisory committee (that may include parents, community members, school and community partner staff) to ensure that they are based on current need.

Conducting a community asset and needs assessment. Information on both needs and assets is gathered intentionally and includes key indicators of student needs (e.g., attendance and academic performance), and family and community needs (e.g., unemployment rates, median income, housing, crime). In addition to formal and informal sources of information related to student, family, and community needs, available resources in the school and community are identified and linked to student and family needs in order to identify gaps in services and potential service areas. Finally, the information from the needs and resource assessment is well-documented in a report and shared with all stakeholders, including partner organizations, school representatives, advisory committee members, potential program providers, students, and parents. Data from the needs assessment are reviewed and updated (annually if not more frequently) to reflect current student, family, and community needs, as well as resources available to address these needs.

Needs and resource assessment is intentionally used to support planning. Community school programming is intentionally designed to address specific student and family needs identified from the need and resource assessment. Analysis of data and linking of needs to resources is conducted by partners, the school, and the advisory committee. Community school programming is intentionally designed to address specific student, family, and community needs identified from the assessment. Stakeholders (e.g., parents, students, partners, school staff) are involved at various levels in the analysis of data and linking of needs to resources.

DOMAIN 2: Establish and maintain community school programs and services.

Family and community program and services are aligned with community and family needs and resources. The services are selected based on a recent and systematic needs and resources assessment, as well as stakeholder input that refines and elaborates on the information reported in the assessment. For example, stakeholders describe schedule preferences and cultural preferences of community members (e.g., need for translators).

Family and community program and services are responsive to community and family needs. Services and how they are provided are closely aligned with community needs. Services are also provided on a schedule that is optimal for community members. Family cultural and language preferences are consistently accommodated by all providers.

Targeted recruitment strategies for students, families and special populations are identified and utilized. The community school has specified the needs of more than one subgroup of family members and has become fully informed about the social, information, and service needs of these populations of family members. Enrollment and participation records for both parents and students—including subgroups of each—are reviewed at multiple points during the school year. Both passive and face-to-face strategies are used to recruit students and family members. Specific and culturally appropriate recruitment strategies have been developed for all student and family subgroups. Participating students and families have a role in encouraging others to participate in activities and services. Recruitment strategies for both students and family members are continually assessed, and new opportunities for recruitment are identified.

DOMAIN 3: Establish and maintain continuous improvement structures.

Identify and collect various sources of information to inform continuous improvement processes. For specific out-of-school programs offered by the Community School, direct observation of quality is conducted using a program/service or school-specific observation tool, along with one or more additional approaches (e.g., surveys, focus groups, interviews, implementation checklists, curriculum review forms). Data inform continuous improvement. For other programs and services (e.g., mental health services, specialized programming), reviews have been conducted that align research-based best practices associated with quality implementation of this program/service, and an implementation checklist is used to monitor adherence to these practices. Data are collected from multiple stakeholders including participants, parents, school-day staff, and Community School program staff.

DOMAIN 4: Develop strategies and commit resources to financially and organizationally sustain the community school.

Establish and maintain relations with key stakeholders to sustain community school activities through active engagement of key stakeholders in planning. Stakeholders (students, families, community partners, and community residents) are informed of community school activities that impact them through newsletters, bulletin boards, fliers, and written communication materials that are differentiated among audiences. Personal communication (e.g., phone calls, meetings) is a primary strategy for communicating with stakeholders.

Establish and maintain relations with key stakeholders to sustain community school activities through school and community outreach. Stakeholders are active participants in planning and implementing activities that impact them. Areas in the community school are available for stakeholders to work/organize. Stakeholders contribute significantly to discussions and plans related to sustainability (e.g., identifying new and existing funding sources, generating ideas for gaining community commitment to the community school). Based on the school and community outreach activities, the school is responsive to the needs of the community and participants and actively looks for ways to be involved in the community (e.g., staff, student or parent volunteer opportunities). The community school utilizes these opportunities to build relationships with potential participants and personnel/providers. Specific and culturally appropriate strategies for establishing/maintaining relationships have been developed for all student and family subgroups.

OUTCOMES

Like all school improvement strategies, steps must be taken to demonstrate the impact community schooling has on a variety of desired outcomes. Most commonly, stakeholders are initially inclined to explore how community schooling has impacted a variety of school-related outcomes, particularly those related to student academic achievement. While it is important, a singular focus on academic achievement ignores the plethora of other ways adoption of community schooling may have benefited enrolled youth, their families, and the community at large. We would argue that the conceptualization of outcomes derived from community schooling needs to be more expansive; aligned to the strategies adopted by the school to address student, family, and community needs; examined in light of the level of strategy implementation reached by the school; and predicated on robust methods and analyses to formulate meaningful impact estimates. In the sections that follow, we first discuss the primary types of outcomes that warrant consideration when developing an evaluation plan to assess the impact of community schooling and then turn our attention to the types of tasks we have employed as part of the evaluation of the Chicago Community Schools Initiative to begin the process of documenting how the initiative has contributed to youth growth and development.

Types of Outcome Data

Generally, data related to examining the impact of community schooling can be broken into three primary categories—(1) direct program outcomes; (2) school-related youth outcomes; and (3) outcomes pertaining to the families of enrolled students and the broader school community.

Direct Program Outcomes

A common thread underpinning most community school efforts is the design and delivery of new programs and services developed to intentionally meet the needs of the school's students in light of results from an assessment of needs and resources. In Chicago, given that a substantial number of community schools receive funding from the federally funded 21st Century Community Learning Centers program (21st CCLC—the largest source of funding for afterschool programming in the country), most schools provide afterschool programs designed to meet the needs of youth attending the community school. As one might imagine, the programming being provided is incredibly diverse, ranging from enrichment offerings providing youth with opportunities to participate in activities in the arts, service learning, or STEM to more overtly academically oriented activities like small-group tutoring or homework help.

Despite this diversity, most programming being provided in CSI schools is designed to support youth development in two primary areas: (1) the development of academic knowledge, attitudes, and behaviors and (2) the development of social and emotional skills and beliefs. Examples of academic knowledge, attitudes, and behaviors may include the following:

- Development of basic, content-specific skills and application of procedural knowledge
- Development of academic-related behaviors and learning strategies (e.g., strategies for monitoring comprehension)
- Cultivation of academic mind-sets (e.g., growth mind-set)
- Cultivation of interest in specific content areas (e.g., STEM)
- Opportunities for deeper learning (e.g., via approaches like project- and inquiry-based learning)

Each of these outcomes helps youth to be better equipped to succeed academically. Examples of outcomes that fall under the umbrella of social and emotional learning include skills and competencies like self-awareness; self-management; interpersonal skills; and strategic thinking and problem-solving skills. SEL skills and competencies have been shown to have a substantive role in supporting a host of school- and workforce-related outcomes (Durlak et al., 2011; Durlak, Weissberg & Pachan, 2010; Farrington et al., 2012).

These types of academic and SEL skills, beliefs, and knowledge are the most immediate outcomes that can emerge from participation in high-quality programming provided at CSI schools. In this sense, youth growth and development across these outcomes happens *within the confines of the program experience* and often can be observed directly by the staff responsible for the design and delivery of activities. As a result, we have dubbed these outcomes *direct program outcomes*.

While these outcomes would seem to be the natural place to start when assessing the impact of community schooling on participating youth, the sheer diversity of program offerings across the schools enrolled in CSI each characterized by a specific and targeted set of outcomes they are trying to impact and the difficulty of finding and using aligned and validated measures has led us to delay action on trying to measure these types of outcomes specifically as part of the evaluation of CSI. We are taking steps currently to create the data collection infrastructure needed to classify schools according to their program delivery focus and the types of outcomes they are trying to achieve in light of the unique set of needs and resources their school has. This will allow for more deliberate efforts in selecting measures and approaches to document how CSI schools are having an impact on direct program outcomes.

Over the span of the next several years, we expect substantial strides will be made generally within the field of education to determine when measurement in this space is viable and develop approaches to assessing youth growth and development on these outcomes. As these developments occur, we will increasingly look to capitalize on these efforts to develop a substantive and meaningful measurement strategy for assessing how enrollment in CSI programming is having an impact on direct program outcomes.

School-Related Outcomes

Using data on school-related outcomes like state assessment scores, school day attendance, and disciplinary incidents are the obvious choices for assessing the impact of community schooling efforts on enrolled youth. As part of the CSI evaluation, we tried to adhere to three general principles in selecting and analyzing data on school-related outcomes: (1) examine those school-related outcomes we anticipated would be impacted by CSI; (2) analyze data separately for key grade-level groupings; and (3) look for impacts among youth spending more time in CSI programs and activities.

In terms of outcome selection, it is important to note that CSI has over 130 schools enrolled in the initiative, making it challenging to determine which specific schools had adopted an approach to community schooling that was likely to drive a specific school-related outcome. While we are heading in a direction in the future that will provide us with the capacity to be more deliberate in selecting those schools likely to move a specific outcome through CSI-related efforts, we did not have this capacity in undertaking the impact analyses we have conducted to date. As a result, we opted to examine a broad array of school-related behavioral and academic outcomes during our initial attempt to explore the impact of the initiative on school-related outcomes.

The domain of outcomes examined varied by grade level. Behavioral outcomes like school-day absences, school-day misconducts, and school-day suspensions were examined for all grade levels. In addition, for students in grades 4–8, state assessment (Illinois Standards Achievement Test–ISAT) reading and mathematics scores were examined, and for students in grades 6–8, various scales obtained from the My Voice, My School survey were also examined. This survey is based on the five essential of effective schools (Bryk et al., 2010) and measures school culture and climate and youth experiences in school and their general well-being. For youth in grades 9–12, academic outcomes like cumulative weighted grade point average (GPA) and the number of credits earned during the year were taken into consideration, as well as the same domain of scales from the My Voice, My School survey utilized in conducting impact analyses for youth in Grades 6–8. Some analyses at this grade level also involved ACT sores and scores from the Illinois state assessment for high school students (Prairie State Achievement Examination–PSAE).

Finally, we also sought to only examine outcomes among youth who had been more intensively involved in programming and activities associated with CSI implementation at the school. For example, "higher dose" students were defined as either attending 60 hours or more of programming both during two consecutive school years or attending 120 hours or more of programming during the school year under examination. When assessing school-related outcomes, it's critical to ensure the student population included in the impact analyses had meaningful and substantive contact with the programming and services delivered as part of community schooling to warrant improvement on the domain of outcomes under consideration.

Family and Community Outcomes

It is fair to say that a community school cannot be deemed successful unless it has created a mutually trusting and beneficial relationship with families and community providers and stakeholders. For CSI, exploring the extent to which a school has met this general goal starts with the concept of leveraged partnerships. Leveraged partnerships represent new providers that the school's CSI resource coordinator recruit to contribute to the community schooling effort based on results from the needs and resources assessment to provide additional, in-kind services to the school. The goal is that leveraged partnerships result in substantive new resources flowing into the school to meet the needs of enrolled students and their families. The concept of leveraged partnerships is at the heart of what the CSI in Chicago is trying to accomplish.

As part of efforts to assess the impact of the initiative on youth outcomes, we took steps to collect data from each school and community partner on the new programming and services provided through leveraged partnerships and the value of those contributions. In schools implementing the Community Schools Model with greater fidelity, the value of programming provided through leveraged partnerships averaged $138,000 for the school year under examination with another $88,000 provided on average in related services (Naftzger, Williams & Liu, 2014). Such results help to both monitor implementation and quantify what the initiative has accomplished in terms of the infusion of new resources into schools serving youth from high-poverty backgrounds.

Another way we have sought to measure the initiative's contribution to community and family involvement has been through school completion of the Continuous Quality Improvement Process (CQIP). As schools go through this process, we have been able to track the extent to which schools take steps to include family and community members in the self-assessment and action planning processes described earlier. In this sense, the CQIP becomes a vehicle for providing family and community members with an active voice in determining what the community school should be, how well it is living up to expectations, and where improvements can be made to better meet the needs of youth and their families. Interviews with family and community members participating in the CQIP have been critical to documenting both how well schools are meeting this outcome and the transformation that is taking place where family and community members are provided a platform to work side-by-side with school staff and providers to create a school that reflects a common and agreed-upon vision.

Finally, we also have been able to leverage existing data collection efforts supported by CPS like the My Voice, My School survey to monitor the extent to which parents feel positive and supported by the school community.

Key Evaluation Tasks Related to Outcomes

One decision each community school initiative needs to make concerns how they are going to approach the collection and analysis of data related to initiative outcomes, when is the right time to conduct these analyses, and how results will be used to support continuous improvement efforts and communicate initiative accomplishments to funders and key stakeholders. In conducting the CSI evaluation, we have used the following principles to guide what key evaluation tasks we perform and when:

Efforts to assess CSI impact should be as robust as possible and lead to the ability to make causal inferences about how the Initiative has impacted youth enrolled at community schools. For CSI, this means conducting a variety of impact analyses using propensity score matching (see Guo & Fraser, 2010, for more details) to create viable comparison groups of youth not enrolled in CSI schools, or in some cases, in lower implementing schools that look as much like youth enrolled in higher implementing CSI schools. Taking careful steps to create viable comparison groups helps ensure that issues of selection bias do not reduce the veracity of impact estimates. Using such methods usually means contracting with a highly skilled local evaluator. Although potentially expensive, this level of rigor is necessary in order to have a high degree of confidence in the validity of impact estimates.

Robust methods to assess impact can be time consuming and costly and therefore should only be conducted (a) when there is evidence that a community school has reached a high level of implementation relative to the CSI Implementation Framework and (b) once every three to four years to determine how impacts may have changed since the last set of impact analyses were completed. The impact analyses we have performed to date were predicated on answering the following set of evaluation questions—to what extent did youth enrolled in programming in higher implementing schools demonstrate better functioning on a variety of academic, behavioral, and learning experience outcomes relative to (a) youth enrolled in programming in lower implementing schools and (b) similar youth attending non-CSI schools?

The comparison with lower implementing schools is directly aligned with the efforts of CSI to develop a series of tools and processes like the CQIP that are oriented toward helping lower-quality community schools progress to higher levels of implementation quality. By answering this question, CPS would have additional information about the possible impact of moving lower implementing schools to a higher level of implementation quality.

The second question was meant to demonstrate the promise of high-implementing community schools in a broader sense by demonstrating the impact the initiative can have relative to similar students enrolled in nonparticipating schools. This information would be helpful to CPS in demonstrating what higher-implementing community schools can achieve in the way of youth outcomes and how these outcomes may justify continued efforts to support the development of effective implementation of the strategy in the full domain of schools enrolled in the initiative.

The viability of assessing these evaluation questions required (a) that implementation quality was defined and operationalized and (b) that a measurement approach was designed and implemented which provided a decent estimate of how schools are doing relative to implementation criteria.

These criteria guided completion of the CSI Impact Report for the 2011–12 school year. Results from the 2011–12 impact report were mixed. Very few differences were found in the outcomes associated with higher and lower implementing schools relative to the CSI Implementation Framework (ISPS). Our hypothesis here is that there were important dynamics of implementation quality that were left unmeasured that may have impacted our results here, most notably the degree of point-of-service quality associated with CSI programming and activities (that is, how supportive, interactive, and engaging CSI programming was for participating youth). Steps have been taken to address this when conducting future impact analyses by formally adopting a point-of-service assessment tool (the short-form Youth Program Quality Assessment) and creating an infrastructure for the collection of these data.

Results from analyses comparing outcomes for "higher dosage" youth in higher implementing schools as compared to similar youth in non-CSI schools were much more promising. In this case, our results indicated that the initiative had a meaningful role in improving student behaviors, specifically reductions in misconducts, suspensions, and unexcused absences and improving youth experiences in school in areas like school belonging, academic personalism, and student-teacher trust. Future analyses will examine the cumulative effect of enrollment in a community school over multiple school years.

Between impact analyses, steps should be taken to monitor school progress on a series of outcome indicators defined for the program. These indicators are meant to help determine if schools are generally on the right track on key outcomes but are not meant to infer that the initiative is causing this growth to occur. Creating the indicators was a collaborative process involving representatives from schools in the Initiative and other key stakeholders. A total of thirty-one indicators have been defined spanning the following outcome areas defined in greater detail by the results framework produced by the national Coalition for Community Schools (CCS, 2008). Citing the interaction of its six "Conditions for Learning," the coalition suggests five short-term results:

• Readiness for School
• Students Attend School Consistently
• Students are Actively Involved in Learning and the Community
• Schools are Engaged with Families and Communities
• Families are Actively Involved in Children's Education
• The framework also indicates four long-term results:

Students Succeed Academically
    Students are Healthy Physically, Socially, and Emotionally
    Students Live and Learn in Stable and Supportive Environments
    Communities are Desirable Places to Live
    Data to populate the indicators comes from the extensive data warehouses maintained by CPS. An infrastructure is currently being developed to allow schools to focus on target indicators they select based on the needs of their school community and linking data on such indicators to the CQIP as a means to add empirical data to the assessment process.

Outcome Conclusions

The most important advice we can offer others about assessing community school efforts is to first and foremost define what effective implementation of the strategy will look like and to have the data collection and analysis pieces in place to know if those implementation targets have been met. Then and only then should serious efforts be made to assess the impact of the initiative on the outcomes the strategy was designed to have an impact on, which may include direct program outcomes, school-related outcomes, and family and community outcomes. Shorter-term outcome indicators can also be defined and used to monitor progress on youth outcomes and support quality improvement efforts, but really should not be used to infer that implementation of the strategy caused desired youth outcomes to happen.

While this chapter has largely focused on evaluation strategies in Chicago, there are other promising community school initiatives that further illustrate practical approaches to evaluating community-focused leadership.

COMMUNITY-FOCUSED LEADERSHIP IN EVANSVILLE, INDIANA

The Evansville Vanderburgh School Corporation (EVSC) has been implementing a community school strategy for over twenty years. Beginning with one full-service school in the early 1990s, the initiative has been scaled throughout the district. In addition, a School Community Council (SCC) emerged to support the district's work. The SCC includes over seventy community partners who are working toward a vision of establishing school sites as places of community to enhance youth and family development. Over the years, several evaluation approaches have been implemented to support community-focused leadership, including measures of implementation and measures of community/school collaboration. To illustrate how community-focused leadership is being evaluated within the EVSC, these approaches are summarized below.

Measuring Implementation

In 2009, the EVSC developed the Essential Framework for Assessing Community School Implementation (Essential Framework). The Essential Framework is grounded in four key assumptions: (1) A community school strategy exists in some manner on a continuum within most schools; (2) While many facets may be deemed as important to distinguishing implementation characteristics, there are essential elements of community schools that provide a foundation for implementation; (3) A defining feature of community schools is the extent to which the school responds to the unique needs/assets of the community which it serves. Since this often leads to variance in implementation, the determination of essential elements of a community school should be jointly influenced by national literature and local experience; and (4) Building- and district-level leadership that supports community schools and the use of formal and informal evaluation are critical to all aspects of implementation and sustainability. Based on these assumptions, eight primary domains serve to define implementation, and each domain contains sub-elements that further illustrate implementation evidence.

While community-focused leadership is integrated within all aspects of the framework, four domains best illustrate this construct. The rationale underlying each of these selected domains is summarized below, along with specific indicators within the domain that support community-focused leadership.

Schools develop formal site councils with a purpose of informing the community school strategy. Site councils include a variety of stakeholders (school staff, parents, community partners) who meet regularly to guide and support the work of the school. Key selected indicators associated with effective site councils include: (a) *Diverse Membership Structures:* The site council composition includes at least one representative from the following groups: school staff member, school building administrator, community organization partner, a school district representative, parent or family member (or someone who represents them), community resident, and youth (or someone who represents them). (b) *Clear Purpose:* The purpose of the site council and expectations for membership are clearly articulated across members.

The school actively works to engage families. The extent to which schools actively work to involve families and engage them in their child's education is an essential practice of community schools. Key selected indicators include (a) the school has implemented strategies based on the formal feedback received from parents (including family surveys and other feedback strategies); and (b) the work of the family engagement team at the school is directly aligned with the school improvement plan.

The school provides programs and services (e.g., social, emotional, and health supports) that are aligned with the unique needs of families, youth, and community members through a Response to Intervention Framework. Community schools provide a variety of supportive services designed to impact students' social, emotional, and health functioning. Key selected indicators include (a) services are aligned to the unique needs of students and families, as opposed to a prescribed one-size-fits-all approach; and (b) a formal process is in place, including data collection, analysis, and interpretation to determine need and resource alignment with need.

A community school strategy is clearly evident within the school's improvement plan demonstrating the connection with student success. A community school strategy should be intentionally integrated within a school's improvement plan. This integration demonstrates the level of commitment on the part of the school in implementing this strategy. Key selected indicators include (a) this integration involves explicit connections of data with community school strategies, as well as evidence of involvement from community partners in this process; (b) the plan includes data from community partners related to the needs of students and families at the school; (c) the school involves community partners in the development of the school improvement plan annually; and (d) there is evidence that the community school strategy is integrated within the school improvement plan.

Measuring School Community Collaboration

Since inception of the School Community Council (SCC), a key evaluation strategy has been assessment of collaborative functioning across partnering community organizations and schools. Toward this aim, the EVSC has administered the Community School Partnership Assessment (Dryfoos and Maguire, 2002) to all community and school partners. The assessment invites partners to rate their agreement on items such as the clarity of the partnership vision, the extent to which results are collaboratively identified, communication among partners, and the mobilization of community resources. In addition, at some schools, individual site councils also administer surveys. These site-level surveys also examine collaborative functioning, but more intently assess the specific partnerships among members of the site council. In all cases, the ongoing assessment of collaborative functioning allows the district and schools to understand the extent to which a high functioning collaborative infrastructure has been established and is being maintained.

In sum, the EVSC's Essential Framework guides schools in implementing community schools, while ongoing collaborative assessments provide the district and schools with a mechanism for ensuring partnerships continue to be meaningful. In doing so, collaborative assessment recognizes that the work is not driven by one entity; rather, it should be a shared endeavor that maximizes the collective impact of all partners. In the context of community-focused leadership, these approaches to evaluation emphasize the critical role that intentional relationships and integrated structures play in the success of community schools.

Chapter Ten

Succession Planning for Community School Leadership— A Personal Reflection

Francisco Borras

At the core of our professional development as principals is the belief in mentorship. As principals we use mentorship to push our teachers farther. The dynamics and interplay of mentorship can play a key role in successive leadership. I believe that in community schools mentorship is critical to safeguarding the successful transition of leadership. While it might not always be the case that a mentorship opportunity can be afforded, it must be proposed as the best-case scenario in order to entertain a more organic and complete plan for succession. Especially given that community school leadership is often a very personal endeavor, and the outreach of a principal is often driven in large part by the principal's personality and character, succession planning is critical for continued success beyond one individual leader. This chapter is based on my experience as the second principal of a very successful community school.

I spent two years as a mentee to the principal who I would eventually succeed, Dr. Carlos Azcoitia, who is coeditor of this book. Dr. Azcoitia had left a legacy in our community, and during his departure, I was linked to the legacy in order to continue trailblazing the pathway for the school and delivering the very best for our children. Dr. Azcoitia was very intentional about handing over the keys to the school. The recipient needed to have "lived" the school, and established strong community ties through the work. While mentorship alone cannot guarantee a seamless transition poised to continue the work of a departing principal, it at least establishes a foundation of relational trust. In community schools, relational trust is the glue that keeps a complex network of stakeholders working together toward a common goal. In this case, Dr. Azcoitia's legacy of transforming a community school into an academic standout within an impoverished and violent Chicago neighborhood had been entrusted to me. While many would have perhaps seen this as a heavy legacy to uphold, trust had emboldened me to succeed.

Mentorship is not about a human vessel pouring knowledge into a waiting receptacle. And it's not about following a golden path and not "erring in my ways." Instead, mentorship is about co-experience and open dialogue, an embracing of the dynamics that lead to reflection and understanding. When I work with teachers on their practice, I never take the stance of having all the answers, and being the one that will impart knowledge to the unknowing. In fact, I stand to learn as much from my teachers as they are from me. It is imperative that the interplay be one of utter respect for the process, and that it is firmly established that we will learn from each other. It is never one-sided. And while there might seem to be a hierarchic relationship at play, it need not be the case, because the roles of both principal and teacher need to be those of learners. I often tell this to my teachers, and make note of it when I see it unfold in the classroom. You are the lead learner in the classroom and, above all, your true role as a teacher is for you to model learning by being an active learner yourself. My mentor was the lead learner, and through our co-learning the plan of succession was born.

The dynamics of mentorship in successive leadership must play out in the public sphere. I remember very clearly that my mentor was very open about everything we discussed. It went beyond transparency. The aim was to showcase the workings of our relationship, and let the community not only spectate but also participate. A lot of our work was done within our local school council. In Chicago, local school councils manage one of the most important stages on which big and decisive decisions are made in order to foster and support the success of schools. Local School Councils are comprised of staff, parents, and community members, and they handle everything from approving yearly school budgets to hiring and firing principals. From the very beginning, I became immersed in the work of the local school council as part of my mentorship. I learned a substantial amount about all the intricacies at play within schools, including budgets and politics, advocacy and compliance, and community voice. In that forum, all stakeholders come together to help guide and govern the school. The principal is there to listen and be one of the guiding voices. They are the lead learner, and they make sure the work is visible for everyone to witness.

As I saw Dr. Azcoitia confronted with the complexities inherit in a community school, I became tuned in to my pressing reality to learn more and quickly. I started to gauge the impact of decisions and became very sensitive to the needs and values of our community. But more notably, what I saw emerge was the deep commitment to a vision—a collective vision. It almost seemed too obvious—100 percent high school and postsecondary graduation.

In 2005, when I first arrived at Spry, tragically, the graduation rate in the Chicago Public Schools hovered just above 50 percent. With its second graduating class, Dr. Azcoitia's final year at Spry, the Class of 2006 posted a graduation rate of 100 percent, the highest of any high school in the district, including selective enrollment schools and charter schools. My mentor was a trailblazer, keenly tied to a vision that everyone was witness to and believed in, and it became a kind of mantra in the community. While in awe of such attainment and deep-rooted convictions, I learned rather quickly that anything other than 100 percent was going to be deemed failure. But still, for me this was both a challenge and opportunity, as I looked to continue the vision but at the same time make it my own.

Over the years I have been able to develop some of the programs that Dr. Azcotia had heralded as instrumental to furthering student opportunities to continue on to college. Such programs gave students the opportunity to have extensive post-secondary experiences before they graduate from high school. We know that by having students have the opportunity to take college coursework while still in high school, they are more apt to continue on to college and graduate. We have established a partnership with two local colleges and universities through which students take coursework for both high school and college credit. Through our University Links program students are able to take college classes in downtown Chicago on Saturday mornings at a local university. Last year, 73 percent of our graduating class attained college-level course credit through either AP or dual college/high school enrollment. For these students college is just the next step, having broken through the barrier that so often keeps students from continuing on to college—not knowing. They begin college with college credit. And the vision continues.

In line with the topic at hand, all students are matched with an adult mentor who helps them navigate their college experience. The vast majority of our students will be the first ones in their families to graduate from high school and go on to college. They don't have anyone in their lives that has taken the steps to college and beyond. For many it is indeed an abrupt awakening, as they are now away from their community and being ushered into a new life of opportunities. The mentors not only serve not as academic tutors but also listen to their stories about failure, success, perseverance, and acknowledge the difficulties of being first-generation college goers. An indeed, these are real college experiences, not specialized programs that simply help expose students to college. They attain credits and grades that become part of their permanent college histories.

Last year we took a giant leap toward enhancing our college-going vision. Through the City Colleges of Chicago we created an extensive Early College program that provides students full-time college experience. Students in their last year of high school can opt to become both full-time high school and college students, taking a full load of college classes. Students take a wide range of courses from calculus to astronomy to sociology and philosophy. As a school we are able to witness first-hand what students struggle with during their first year of college. We have gained invaluable knowledge from this program as it has served to better inform our school decisions on how to better prepare our students for college. If as a school community we didn't have a commitment to the vision of 100 percent postsecondary graduation, I don't think we would be able to sustain such programs. Indeed, the tremendous challenges that come with these programs are only overcome because of our strong collective belief in our school's vision.

The vision is greater than just one individual whose role is to disseminate and herald it for the community. Because my mentor had instilled the commitment to this vision in our school community, it was passed over to me as a blazing torch. I had been witness to how the vision had been developed and embraced, and substantiated by building the capacity of all stakeholders, including teachers, students, and parents, to uphold it. I was never handed a road map as to how to carry and navigate with the torch, but the message was clear: keep the torch ablaze.

To this day what has resonated within me the most, and helped me frame my work, has been the commitment to our community that my mentor heralded from the very beginning. We are a community school trying to weather the harsh reality of funding woes, including the proliferation of charter schools that siphon funding and students from our schools. Despite all the obstacles, we stand as a beacon in the community committed to the holistic welfare of our students and their families. I remember well that on the eve of my mentor's departure, he had helped organize efforts to bring a school-based health clinic to our school. This was such an important chapter in our school's history since it helped expand our mission to educate our students not only within our classrooms, but within the context of our community as a whole. We are committed to the whole child. While academics stands tall within our school's vision, we also take great measures to guarantee the safety and well-being of our students and their families. We know that without this commitment we can never truly maximize the learning of our students. The clinic was a first step. We now partner with other community agencies to provide resources for our students and their families, everything from shelter to help with immigration proceedings to work placements for our students. We believe strongly that by creating a strong and expansive network of community resources for our families, we are better able to support our students' education within our classrooms. This is a core belief.

In successive leadership within schools immediate attention needs to be given to the core beliefs of a school, and the new leader needs to be privy to how those beliefs resonate with their own system of beliefs. A prime example are the beliefs pertaining to going to college. We can easily take up the

100 percent postsecondary graduation torch, but what does it mean within our community? We often forget the harsh realities that accompany our first-generation college goers' decision to take the steps toward college. The realities of financial strains, navigating bureaucratic systems, lack of diversity on campus, language and cultural barriers all come together and quickly deflate the spirit of college. Therein lies my struggle. At the end of the day college is big business, and more often than not is simply a societal sorting game for the sake of perpetuating the disenfranchisement of our students. During my first year on the job I remember sending five of our top students to a highly selective university, only to have them jettisoned and literally thrown to the curb after having incurred thousands of dollars of debt. The majority of the students were undocumented, and the university had little in the way of resources to support them. The university simply did not care. One of the students survived miraculously, persevered heroically, and is now a teacher in our community. Unfortunately, that narrative does not play out very often.

Despite the atrocities that are blindly committed by institutions like colleges and universities, advocating for 100 percent postsecondary graduation is still at the heart of our work within our school. And this is why, and this might sound a bit idealistic and sanctimonious, the opportunity of college is about giving our students the experience of learning for learning's sake. It might seem like a naïve stance, but having students fall in love with learning is the only vehicle toward eradicating barriers of access to the ivory tower. Yes, they will have to deal with all the harshness, but the fruit of their labor will help them push through life knowing that no one and nothing can ever take away their passion for learning. That is what we need to promote, not going to college for college's sake.

Neither passive acceptance nor tabula rasa of a vision will accomplish the end goal, which is the continued advancement of the school. It needs to be internalized and reconfigured by the new leader. The vision of 100 percent high school and postsecondary graduation has continued to burn strongly within our school ever since Dr. Azcoitia left the school nine years ago. That vision continues to be owned by the community, and it has been my job to continue to develop the capacity in all stakeholders to sustain it.

Only trust and transparency and commitment to learning can guarantee the successful transition of a school's leadership. Over the past nine years I have seen our community high school evolve, but it took a strong foundation and commitment from the very beginning to give it life. We mentor our children as parents, educators, and community members, and it is our mission to make sure children know that that is how we ultimately learn, from each other, through dialogue, sharing, listening, and acting. Spry Community Links High School continues to thrive today because of that very mission, passed along from mentor to future mentor.

References

Algebra Project, Inc. (2005). A campaign for quality education as a civil right. Memorandum to Participants in the First Algebra Project Network Conference on Quality Education, Howard University, Washington, D.C.

Berzonsky, M. D., and L. S. Kuk. (2005). Identity style, psychosocial maturity, and academic performance. *Personality & Identity Differences, 39*(1), 235–247.

Blank, M., A. Berg, and A. Melaville. (2006). *Growing community schools: The role of cross boundary leadership*. Washington, D.C.: Coalition for Community Schools, Institute for Educational Leadership.

Blank, M. J., A. Melville, and B. P. Shah. (2003). *Making the difference: Research and practice in community schools*. Washington, D.C.: Coaltion for Community Schools.

Block, P. (2009). *Community*. San Francisco: Berrett-Koehler Publishers.

Boykin, A. W., and P. Noguera. (2011). *Creating the opportunity to learn: Moving from research to practice*. Alexandria: ASCD.

Bryk, A. S., P. B. Sebring, E. Allensworth, S. Luppescu, and J. Q. Easton. (2010). *Organizing schools for improvement: Lessons from Chicago*. Chicago, IL: University of Chicago Press.

Bryk, A., and B. Schneider. (2002). *Trust in schools: A core resource for improvement*. New York: Russell Sage Foundation.

Chang, H. N., and M. Romero. (2008). *Present, engaged and accounted for: The critical importance of addressing chronic absence in the early grades*. New York: National Center for Children in Poverty, Columbia University.

Children's Aid Society. (2011). *Building community schools: A guide to action*. New York: Author.

Coalition for Community Schools (2008). *Community schools: Promoting student success. A rationale and results framework*. Washington, DC: Author.

Coalition for Community Schools (n.d.). *What is a community school?* Available at http://www.communityschools.org/aboutschools/what_is_a_community_school.aspx.

Comer, J. (1980). *School power: Implications of an intervention project*. New York: Free Press.

Comer, J. (1988). *Maggie's American dream: The life and times of a black family*. New York: New American Library.

Comer, J. (2009). *What I learned in school: Reflections on race, child development, and school reform*. San Francisco: Jossey-Bass.

Comer, J. P., N. M. Haynes, E. T. Joyner, and M. Ben-Avie. (1996). *Rallying the whole village: The Comer process for reforming education*. New York, NY: Teachers College Press.

Council of Chief State School Officers (2015). ISLLC 2015: Model policy standards for educational leaders. Draft for public comment: May 11, 2015–May 29, 2015.

Cox-Peterson, A., L. R. Melber, and T. R. Patchen. (2012). *Teaching science to culturally and linguistically diverse elementary students.* Upper Saddle River, NJ: Pearson.

Dewees, S. (1999). *Improving rural school facilities for teaching and learning.* Charleston: ERIC Clearinghouse on Rural Education and Small Schools.

Dual Capacity Building Framework for Family School Partnerships issued by the Department of Education http://www2.ed.gov/documents/family-community/partners-education.pdf.

Duncan, G., and R. Murnane. (2014). Growing income inequality threatens American education. *Education Week,* published online March 28, 2014. Available at http://www.edweek.org/ew/articles/2014/03/01/kappan_duncanmurnane.html.

Durlak, J. A., R. P. Weissberg, and M. Pachan. (2010). A meta-analysis of after-school programs that seek to promote personal and social skills in children and adolescents. *American Journal of Community Psychology, 45,* 294–309.

Durlak, J., A. B. Dymnicki, R. D. Taylor, R. Weissberg, and K. B. Schellinger. (2011). The impact of enhancing students' social and emotional learning: A meta-analysis of school based universal interventions. *Child Development, 82*(1), 405–432.

Dymond, J. A. (2014). Strategic community engagement as perceived by five superintendents. Doctoral dissertation completed at National Louis University, Chicago, IL.

Farrington, C. A., M. Roderick, E. Allensworth, J. Nagaoka, T. S. Keyes, D. W. Johnson, et al. (2012). *Teaching adolescents to become learners. The role of noncognitive factors in shaping school performance: A critical literature review.* Chicago, IL: The University of Chicago Consortium on Chicago School Research.

Federal Register (2010). Feb. 8, 2010, p. 6188.

Gardner, J. (1993). *On leadership.* New York: Free Press.

Glanz, G. (2006). *What every principal should know about school-community leadership.* Thousand Oaks, CA: Corwin Press.

Guo, S., and M. W. Fraser. (2010). *Propensity score analysis: Statistical methods and applications.* Thousand Oaks, California: Sage Publications Inc.

Hanley, M. S., and G. W. Noblit. (2009). *Cultural responsiveness, racial identity and academic success: A review of literature.* Pittsburgh: The Heinz Endowments.

Harackiewicz, J. M., K. E. Barron, and A. J. Elliot. (1998). Rethinking achievement goals: When are they adaptive for college students and why? *Educational Psychologist, 33*(1), 1–21.

Henderson, A., and K. Mapp. (2002). *A new wave of evidence.* Austin, TX: SEDL.

Jehl, J., M. J. Blank, and B. McCloud. (2001). *Education and community building: Connecting two worlds.* Southwest Educational Development Laboratory. Washington, DC: Institute for Educational Leadership.

Jimerson, L. (2003). *The competitive disadvantage: Teacher compensation in rural America.* Arlington: The Rural School and Community Trust.

Kilduff, M., and D. V. Day. (1994). Do chameleons get ahead? The effects of self-monitoring on managerial careers. *Academy of Management Journal, 37*(4), 1047–1060.

Kretzmann, J., and J. McKnight. (1993). *Building communities from the inside out: A path toward finding and mobilizing a community's assets.* Evanston, IL: The Asset-Based Community Development Institute, Institute for Policy Research, Northwestern University.

Lopez, M. E. (2003). *Transforming schools through community organizing: A research review.* Cambridge, MA: Harvard Family Research Project.

Losen, D., and R. Skiba. (2010). *Suspended education.* Montgomery, AL: Southern Poverty Law Center.

Mapp, K. L., and P. J. Kuttner. (2013). *Partners in education: A dual capacity-building framework for family-school partnerships.* Austin, TX: SEDL.

Martinez, L., and C. Hayes. (2013). *Measuring social return on investment in community schools: A case study.* New York: The Children's Aid Society.

Marzano, R. J. (2003). What works in schools. Alexandria: ASCD.

Meece, J. L., P. C. Blumenfeld, and R. H. Hoyle. (1988). Students' goal orientations and cognitive engagement in classroom activities. *Journal of Educational Psychology, 80*(4), 514–523.

Meier, D. (2002). *In schools we trust: Creating communities of learning in an era of testing and standardization.* Boston: Beacon Press.

Naftzger, N., R. William, and F. Liu. (2014). *Chicago Public Schools Community Schools Initiative Evaluation: 2011–12 Impact Report.* Chicago, IL: American Institutes for Research.

National Center for Community Schools. (2011). *Building community schools: A guide for action.* New York: The Children's Aid Society.

National Policy Board for Educational Administration (2015). *Professional standards for educational leaders 2015.* Reston, VA: Author.

Payne, C. (2008). *So much reform, so little change: The persistence of failure in urban schools.* Cambridge, MA: Harvard Education Press.

Perry, C. A. (1912). *Social center features in new elementary school architecture and the plans of sixteen socialized schools.* New York City: Division of recreation, Russell Sage Foundation.

Purinton, T. (2011). *Six degrees of school improvement: Empowering a New Profession of Teaching.* Charlotte, NC: IAP.

Putnam, R. (2015). *Our kids: The American dream in crisis.* New York: Simon & Schuster.

Saenz, V. B., S. Hurtado, D. Barrera, D. Wolf, and F. Yeung. (2007). *First in my family: A profile of first-generation college students at four-year institutions since 1971.* Los Angeles: Higher Education Research Institute.

Sebring, P. B., and A. S. Bryk, et al. (2000). School leadership and the bottom line in Chicago. *Phi Delta Kappan, 81,* 440–443.

Shama, D., and K. A. McTavish. (2009). Making room for place-based knowledge in rural classrooms. *Rural Educator, 30*(2), 1–4.

Singleton, G. E., and C. Linton. (2006). *Courageous conversations about race. A field guide for achieving equity in schools.* Thousand Oaks, CA: Corwin Press.

Southern Education Foundation (2015). A new majority: Low income students now a majority in the nation's public schools. Atlanta: Author.

Southwest Rural Health Research Center (2010). Rural healthy people 2010 project. College Station, TX: Author.

Stern, J. D. (1994). *The condition of education in rural schools.* Washington, DC: U.S. Government Printing Office.

Superville, D. R. (2015). New school leaders' standards released for public comment. *Education Week,* September 15, 2015.

Terrell, R. D., and R. B. Lindsay. (2009). *Culturally proficient leadership: The personal journey begins within.* Thousand Oaks, CA: Corwin Press.

U.S. Census Bureau (2010). *State and county quick facts.* Available at http://quickfacts.census.gov/qfd/states/23/23031.html.

United Way (2008). *Goals for the common good: United Way's challenge to America.* Alexandria, VA: Author.

Vogel, L. R. (March 2002). Leading with hearts and minds: Ethical orientations of educational leadership doctoral students. Values and Ethics in Educational Administration, Vol.10, No. 1. Centre for the Study of Leadership and Ethics. New Zealand: UCEA, pp.1–12.

Was, C. A., I. Al-Harthy, M. Stack-Oden, and R. M. Isaacson. (2009). Academic identity status and the relationship to achievement goal orientation. *Electronic Journal of Research in Educational Psychology, 7*(2), 627–652.

Weick, K. E. (1976). Educational organizations as loosely coupled systems. *Administrative Science Quarterly, 21*(1), 1–19.

Welch, O. M., and C. R. Hodges. (1997). *Standing outside on the inside: Black adolescents and the construction of academic identity.* Albany: SUNY Press.

Whalen, S. P. (2002). *Report of the evaluation of the Polk Bros. Foundation's Full Service Schools Initiative.* Chicago, IL, University of Chicago, Chapin Hall Center for Children.

Whalen, S. P. (2007). *Three years into Chicago's Community Schools Initiative (CSI): Progress, challenges, and emerging lessons.* Chicago: College of Education, University of Illinois at Chicago.

Williams, D. T., and J. Johnson. (2002). *Rural school leadership in the deep South: The double-edged legacy of school desegregation.* Arlington: The Rural School and Community Trust.

Wilson, J. Q. (1991). *Bureaucracy: What government agencies do and why they do it.* New York: Basic Books.

Winton, S., and K. Pollock. (2013). Preparing politically savvy principals in Ontario, Canada. *Journal of Educational Administration, 51*(1), 40–54.

Zander, K., E. Burnside, and M. Poff. (2011). *The Development of an implementation and sustainability process strategy (ISPS) for the Chicago Public Schools Community Schools Initiative: Findings and recommendations.* Chicago: Chicago Public Schools Office of Student Support and Engagement.

Index

About the Contributors

Carlos Azcoitia is Distinguished Professor of Practice at National Louis University in Chicago. Azcoitia previously was the Founding Principal of a new "Comprehensive Community School" concept on Chicago's Little Village Neighborhood. He previously served as the Deputy Chief of Education in the Chicago Public Schools. His doctorate is from Northern Illinois University. Azcoitia actively contributes to several boards, assisting them in a meaningful, hands-on capacity. He was appointed by the mayor to serve on the Chicago Board of Education and is Chair of the Board of Trustees at Northeastern Illinois University. Dr. Azcoitia is a Steering Committee Member of the Coalition of Community Schools in Washington DC. He is a Board Member of the Chicago High School for the Arts and Ignatian Spirituality Center in Miami. Dr. Azcoitia is the author of many published articles about school reform.

Martin Blank has been the president of the Institute of Educational Leadership (IEL) since 2009. He leads IEL in its mission to equip leaders to work together across boundaries to build effective systems that prepare children and youth for college, careers, and citizenship. Blank has been associated with IEL since 1985, focusing his work on building bridges between schools and other institutions with assets that can support student success. He also serves as the Director of the Coalition for Community Schools, which is staffed by the Institute for Educational Leadership. The Coalition is a network of organizations and institutions at the local, state, and national levels working to unite school and communities. Blank stays involved with local activities in the District of Columbia. He is the former Chair of D.C. VOICE, an education reform collaborative, and of the Management Team of the Early Childhood Collaborative. He has a BA from Columbia University, 1965, and a JD from Georgetown University Law Center. He served as a VISTA Volunteer in the Missouri Bootheel.

Francisco Borras is Principal of Spry Community Links High School on the southwest side of Chicago. The school program entails wraparound services that support academics, social-emotional learning, and community empowerment. At the school, he leads various projects that include a public library, a school-based clinic, a community play garden, and an Early College program.

Chris Brown is the Director of Education and Engagement at the Local Initiatives Support Corporation (LISC) in Chicago. In this position he oversees the Elev8 program, an effort to transform five middle schools in Chicago through academic, health, social support, and community organizing programming. He also works on LISC Chicago's other education initiatives and seeks to increase the capacity of LISC's partners to engage stakeholders in their work. Previously he consulted with nonprofits and foundations on issues related to education and community organizing, was the Education Program Officer at the Steans Family Foundation, directed the Schools and Communities program at the Cross City Campaign for Urban School Reform, was the Community Development Program Officer at the United Way, and was a community organizer with ACORN. In addition to his professional work, he founded and was the first chairperson of the West Rogers Park Community Organization and has chaired the Jones College Prep and Boone Elementary Local School Councils.

Karen Glinert Carlson is associate professor and chair of Educational Leadership Programs at Dominican University, River Forest, Illinois. In this role, Carlson prepares aspiring school leaders. She also coaches and mentors aspiring and novice principals through the Chicago Leadership Collaborative. Carlson spent thirty-four years in public education, serving as a bilingual teacher, bilingual special education teacher, special education supervisor, principal of two different award-winning community schools in Chicago, Executive Director of the Chicago Schools Academic Accountability Council, Director of Special Education, Associate Superintendent of Waukegan School District 60, and Superintendent of School District 92 in Broadview, IL. She also worked for Chicago's business community at the Civic Committee and served as a policy analyst, program developer, and advisor to the Chicago Board of Education. Carlson serves on a number of boards and civic organizations and is a fellow of Leadership Greater Chicago. She has received many awards and recognition for her work, especially her work developing Prescott School into a thriving community school being noted as a Dewitt Wallace Readers Digest American Hero in Education, Phi Delta Kappa Educator of the Year, and having a proclamation and day named in her honor in Illinois. She has presented and consulted with districts and schools across the country.

Daniel Diehl is the President of Diehl Consulting Group (DCG), an evaluation firm with extensive experience in evaluating full-service community school initiatives. DCG partners with the American Institutes for Research on the multiyear evaluation of the Chicago Public Schools Community Schools Initiative. In this role, DCG supports measurement of community school implementation and is a member of the Evaluation Advisory Group. Dr. Diehl is a former director of community learning centers with the Evansville Vanderburgh School Corporation (EVSC), and current cochair of the EVSC School Community Council Evaluation Committee. He is also a founding member of the Indiana Afterschool Network.

Judith Dymond is Coordinator for the Northern Illinois University (NIU) Center for Economic Education and is an Outreach & Engagement Associate for STEM Outreach. Dymond specializes in connecting K–12 schools to the university through professional development for economic educators and through leading the STEM Café program which connects adults and students to the university. She has served as K–12 Director of Instructional Services, Assistant Special Education Director, Title Grants Coordinator, Assistant Middle School Principal, and Reading Specialist. She holds a doctorate in Educational Leadership from National Louis University and a Master's in Curriculum and Instruction from University of Wisconsin–Madison. Judith is passionate about connecting schools to the university and other community resources.

Neil Naftzger is a principal researcher working on afterschool and expanded learning initiatives at American Institutes for Research (AIR). An experienced evaluator and researcher within the field of after-school programs, Naftzger has spent more than a decade designing and conducting evaluations and research studies in the after-school and extended learning time arena that involve the collection and analysis of data in various forms, particularly in relation to the 21st Century Community Learning Centers (21st CCLC) program. Naftzger studies both the impact of youth-serving programs on various outcomes and the role program quality plays in this process. Naftzger has been the principal investigator on research grants from the Charles Stewart Mott and William T. Grant Foundations and on statewide evaluations of the 21st CCLC programs in New Jersey, Ohio, Oregon, Texas, and Washington. Naftzger also is leading a multiyear evaluation of the Community School Initiative administered by Chicago Public Schools and a study funded by the

National Science Foundation to study how youth interest and engagement develop in STEM-oriented summer learning programs.

Ted Purinton is Dean of the Graduate School of Education at the American University in Cairo (AUC). As dean, he leads an influential faculty in the areas of higher education policy, educational administration, and comparative and international education. The faculty of his school is actively involved in reform and research for schools, universities, governments, NGOs, multilateral organizations, and other educationally related institutions. Before AUC, Purinton was chair of the Department of Educational Leadership at National Louis University in Chicago, as well as Assistant Professor in that department. As chair, Purinton initiated partnerships with charter school networks, local school coalitions, teacher union reform networks, and other groups to increase the university's influence on school leadership preparation. He also worked closely with local and state governments on school finance reform, as well as on teacher and school leader preparation reform. Purinton holds a doctorate in educational policy and administration from the University of Southern California.

Adeline Ray is Senior Manager for the Chicago Public Schools (CPS) Community Schools Initiative (CSI). Having transformed over two hundred schools into vibrant centers of their communities, she oversees all aspects of the initiative for CPS including grant development and reporting, strategic implementation, evaluation design and data sharing. Ms. Ray was honored in 2016 with the Coalition for Community Schools' Community Schools Initiative Leadership Award. She serves on the Illinois State Board of Education's 21st CCLC Professional Development Advisory Group and THRIVE Chicago; is an active member of the Coalition for Community Schools' Steering Committee and co-chairs the Coalition's Community Schools Leadership Network.

Mary A. Ronan has led Cincinnati Public Schools to the distinction of being Ohio's highest-performing urban school district for four consecutive school years. Ronan's priorities have been to enhance collaboration and transparency while accelerating academic achievement. She introduced new strategies designed to increase student performance, including My Tomorrow*ed, which envisions, within six years, 100 percent of all district seventh graders will graduate prepared to actively pursue their chosen career path; and, the Elementary Initiative: Ready for High School which provides intensive support at the district's sixteen lowest-performing elementary schools. At the high school level, Ronan focuses on increasing the academic rigor of course offerings and expending college access. A believer in the power of partnerships, Ronan has expanded the district's nationally recognized Community

Learning Centers model to forty-three schools as of fall of 2015. These Community Learning Centers act as hubs that operate beyond the traditional school day to provide academic, health, recreational, and enrichment supports to students, families, and neighborhoods.

Doris Terry Williams directs both the Leadership Council and the Capacity Building Program of the Rural School and Community Trust (Rural Trust), based in Arlington, Virginia. Formerly the Annenberg Rural Challenge, the Rural Trust is the premier national nonprofit organization addressing the crucial relationship between good rural schools and thriving rural communities. Williams guides and oversees the organization's work with a network that has numbered more than seven hundred rural schools and communities in thirty-five states, strengthening their capacity to improve together and to make rural places good places to live, work, and learn. She has led the Trust's Stewards Program as it transitioned from grants making to capacity building; overseen the development and field testing of an assessment system for place-based, project-based, and service learning in partnership with the Educational Testing Service (ETS) and Rural Trust field sites; and designed a rural school leadership development initiative for the Deep South. In addition, she leads the Rural Trust's efforts at rural high school reform, its Rural Teacher Development Center, and its Education Renewal Zones initiative. Previously Assistant Dean and Associate Professor at the North Carolina Central University School of Education and Director of University-School Partnerships, Williams led the institution's teacher education program reform. Williams co-founded, and subsequently directed, the North Carolina Center for the Study of Black History. She established two programs for young people in Warren County, North Carolina: the Warren Service Corps; and the Warren Summer Scholars Program. She has also been lead consultant and trainer for several state and national school and community reform efforts, and has authored a community economic development training manual for the Southern Initiative of the Algebra Project. Williams' experience also includes ten years as director of a regional adult literacy program and twelve years of service on the Warren County Board of Education, five as Board chairperson. Williams holds an EdD and MEd from North Carolina State University and an AB from Duke University.